INTO DISREPUTE

THE INVENTIVE COMIC OPERA OF 1970'S POLICING

NEIL MACH

Into Disrepute

Neil Mach

© Copyright November 30th 2016

The right of Neil Mach to be identified as author of this work has been asserted by him in accordance with the Copyright, Designs and Patents Act 1988.

All Rights Reserved

No reproduction, copy or transmission of this publication may be made without written permission. No paragraph of this publication may be reproduced, copied, or transmitted save with the written per-mission of the publisher, or in accordance with the provisions of the Copyright Act 1956 (as amended.)

Any person who does any unauthorised act in relation to this publication may be liable to criminal prosecution and civil claims for damage.

A CIP catalogue record for this title is available from the British Library.

First Published in eBook form 2016

Cover art by © Neil Mach with thanks to toddhatten

Ink by Neil Mach. Author site: https://maxwritivity.club/

❦ Created with Vellum

To Petey and Ruth
And everyone who lived at Square 28 1975-1980
This book is also dedicated to every officer
who served on 'Q Division' in the 1970's
But especially Bernie,
Bernie he is the hero

2

Duty Statement

I have been asked to complete a statement describing the events leading up to the discipline hearing of P.C. Rufus Palmerston. I have been asked to include details of my knowledge of the Constable's character and describe his behavior during my time spent with him at Quebec Mike police station during the summer and autumn of 1975.

This statement consisting of 325 pages (each signed by me) is accurate to the best of my knowledge and belief. I make it knowing that if it is tendered in evidence, I shall be liable to prosecution if I have willfully stated in it anything which I know to be false or do not believe to be true.

This is my true recollection of each episode. The evidence I give here is still fresh in my memory. I apologize in advance for coarse or offensive language that I have used or repeated when making this official duty statement. Where I have used profanities or vulgar words or jargon/slang it is because I have contemporaneously recorded such exchanges in my pocket notebook. Notes were made at the time of each event, or as soon after as reasonably practicable.

3

4

The Stewart Granger

On Monday 26th May 1975, I commenced a scheduled Early Turn shift, starting at 06:00, at 'Quebec' Mike police station. It would be my initial tour at the station, newly transferred-in from C Division, West End Central. I had recently been promoted to the rank of Police Sergeant (probationary.)

The first 'Q' division Constable I glimpsed on my new posting was Constable Godfrey Lambert. I observed Godfrey wore the Police Long Service and Good Conduct ribbon on his tunic. The medal indicated he had completed at least 22 years police service.

'We've got a jumper,' Godfrey told me. As he sauntered across the yard, he munched on a slice of Sunblest toast. He arrived at the doors of an Austin 1100 Panda car. Flecks of marmalade attached themselves to his greying moustache and the gold shreds matched the hues and textures of the dry gunk around his eyes. Dandruff flecked his shoulders, and his shirt had a raunchy two-day aroma. The pang of B.O. could be detected five steps away. Godfrey did not believe in splashing *Brut* all-over.

'Off a railway bridge?' I enquired.

'Yup,' he said. 'It's as good today as it's always been.'

I also saw a tall, red-headed Constable. This Constable wobbled into view and offered me a skeptical smile. He had watchful, chestnut eyes, pink eyelashes, and a rosy face. He was quite a large man, flabby around the middle, with hefty shoulders and oversized buttocks. I now know this man to be Constable Rufus Palmerston — identified by all his colleagues as: 'Ruff.' He is the subject of my disciplinary investigation and will be the focus of this duty statement.

'Good to the last drop,' Ruff sang, with a grin. He drained the last dregs from a bottle of Teacher's Scotch, held in his left hand.

'That's what I said,' Godfrey Lambert told Ruff. The older Constable licked his lips to show his approval, then chuckled.

'Quick change-over last night,' Ruff clarified, when he glanced my way. 'Late turn yesterday. We got off duty at midnight. Me and the old-timer stayed at the nick. Had a card game. Then drank a bottle.'

'You slept here?' I asked.

'Had a couple of hours in the boiler room. Not so bad once you're used to the scampering of rats. And the spiders get up your nose. I don't know what Godfrey did. He probably got his head down in the lady's loo, that's his favorite. Not likely to be disturbed there —'

I saw that P.C. Godfrey had managed to jiggle-open the driver's door on his chosen Panda: 'What kind of idiot-bastard locked this thing?' he grumbled. 'I told those masturbatory nob-jockeys on late turn *not* to lock the jam-jars. They're a bunch of tosspots.' He slid into the front seat and started the engine with a roar. Satisfied, he struck a long Vesta match and watched the chemicals burn. Once the head stopped flaring, he put the flame into his pipe. 'There's nothing like starting your day the Kellogg's fucking way,' he said, as he puffed.

Meanwhile, a separate Panda roared from the courtyard. This one, also an Austin 1100, whizzed away — cut past us — with inches to spare. I later discovered *this* Panda was driven by Constable 120Q Martin Duke — also known, moderately affectionately, as 'Farting Martin.' On that morning Fart'n Mart'n was assigned to Panda Two.

'Twat —' we uttered in unison, as we watched the Panda speed out of the yard.

'See you there, Grandpops,' Ruff told Godfrey.

'Right-oh sonny,' grinned the older man. He yanked his door shut and crashed the Austin into first gear. He stamped on the accelerator with such force we could hear the clunk of pedal-to-metal *outside* the vehicle. Then the old man's Panda roared away.

I strolled across the station yard with Ruff Palmerston. He directed me to the station van. 'Haven't had a cuppa yet,' he grumbled. He finished a Benson and Hedges ciggie and slung it onto the asphalt along with the empty whisky bottle. He made no effort to place the trash into a receptacle situated near the canteen door.

'They get onto the bridge to fuck themselves early —' he explained. 'They crap-up the lives of regular folk.' It took me several moments to realize he talked about *jumpers*. 'I don't mind them dispatching themselves,' Ruff continued 'But why do they have to involve everyone else in their wretched business?'

'I've never been to a jumper before,' I said.

'Where are you from Sarge?'

'West End Central.'

'Well, there you are then. Not many jumpers down in the smoke.'

'We get our fair share of one-unders —' I told him.

'Yes. I expect that you do.'

We leapt into the Transit van, with Ruff dumping his huge buttocks onto the driving seat. It rumbled to life. Ruff clattered the vehicle out of the back yard.

'Click on the radio, would you Skip?'

I fired up the main-set.

'Do the honours...'

I located the microphone. It resembled a grey electric razor. I resisted the urge to rub it against my morning stubble. 'MP, MP from Quebec Mike Two. Are you receiving?'

'Go ahead Quebec Mike Two.'

'Show us on the air oh-six hundred hours. On the way to a bridge jumper. Section sergeant on board. Ps 76Q.'

5

It took less than five minutes to reach Suicide Bridge.

Two pandas were already on the scene. I noted that two early turn Constables had put in roadblocks and started to the re-route commuter flow. Plenty of rush-hour traffic had started to queue.

I discerned that the wireless car — call sign Quebec Six — had been parked near the rail embankment. I learnt later that the wireless car I saw at that time (or area car, as it's officially known) was still manned by night duty staff. They don't swap over crews till 07:00.

Ruff Palmerston mounted the kerb, then drove the station van along the footpath. He by-passed a line of traffic and scared the shit out of early-morning dog walkers, who yanked their pets onto the grass verge to avoid them being splattered. He pulled up behind the blue Rover using an unnecessary handbrake stop.

I remarked that it started to drizzle. Though Constable Palmerston ignored me. 'Come and talk to Uncle Rufus,' he said, apparently to himself. He took a long drag on a newly ignited cigarette. Then rolled the driver's window to allow a small portion of smoke to escape. 'Let's go Larky. Don't you want to go home to sleepy-bye land? I haven't got all day. You scrawny fucker.'

The door of the wireless car gradually opened, and I saw an underfed Constable uncoil himself from the front seat and saunter towards our van. The undernourished Constable went to Ruff's side of the vehicle.

'Morning mate,' said the thin Constable. 'We haven't been up there yet. The call came in just then. So, we waited for you.'

Ruff ignored him. Instead, he made a hammy rubbernecking movement towards my side of the van. 'Have you met our new *Sergeant*, Larky?' he shouted, theatrically.

The youthful Constable gazed through the cloud of cigarette smoke and recognized I had been sitting in the van, wearing three stripes, all along. 'Sarge, this is Constable Lark from 'A' relief. He is an ignorant fuck,' Ruff muttered, by way of introduction.

'Sorry, Skip, I didn't see you there,' the Constable shouted. He came around my side of the vehicle. 'Apologies for that, Skipper. Yes, I don't know how much you know about this, but I'm happy to fill you in. Basically, there's an old Paki up on the railway bridge. British Rail informed us, and they have done everything necessary their end. They stopped the choo-choos. I think your boys closed the road. While the L.F.B. are over in the pub car park. Ambulance on its way. I don't know anything about the *Reg Varney* yet. We can partially see the geezer, though. He's standing about halfway across the bridge. Anything else you want us to do?'

I shook my head. Then glanced at Ruff Palmerston to check he seemed happy with my decision.

'We'll take it from here, Larky,' Ruff said. 'Go and get your beauty sleep, sunshine. And don't wank too hard...'

'Thanks, mate. Thanks, Skip. I am cream-crackered as it happens. Leave it to you guys, then?'

6

'Better see the man on the bridge,' Ruff said as the early urn wireless car did a dangerous 3-point turn and roared off. P.C. Palmerston flicked his finished dog-end onto the verge then stuffed the van keys under the sun-visor. 'Turn off the radio would you sunshine? Or it will drain the battery to cock.'

I asked Ruff why we didn't lock the police vehicle.

'Who is going to fucking nick it?' he remarked. 'In any case, if you need to return — maybe because I am 'indisposed' — at least you'll know you can open up and get going.'

This explanation made sense, I suppose — though I told Constable Palmerston that it would be very unwise to leave a police vehicle unlocked and unattended in Central London, on 'C' Division. 'It would be trashed if we left our van unlocked in Leicester Square, for example,' I told him.

'Welcome to Q division,' he replied. 'The population round here can be trusted — they actually *like* the police... unlike those shits in Soho and Savile Row.'

I accidentally broke wind as I bounded from the van into the light morning rain.

'Good morning, good morning / the best to you each morning...' Ruff sang melodiously, as my fart echoed under the bridge.

'I have never dealt with a jumper before.' I told him.

'Yes, you already said that.' Ruff gazed at me. 'There's nothing to it. Either way, he comes down. In both cases, we need to inform his next of kin. In both cases, we need to write out a bloody report. In both cases, it's a waste of everyone's fucking time.'

'In both cases, we need to inform his next of kin?'

'Yeah. Because either he jumps, or he doesn't. And if he doesn't fucking jump —we nick him. Under the Mental Health Act, don't we? Do you see? We get him sectioned. So, we'll need to tell his folks if he's going to the loony bin, yeah? If we don't nick him, he'll come back and try again. So, we always nick them, or we scrape them. Either way, we need to inform next of kin. Let's hope today is *not* a scraping day.'

'I see.'

'That reminds me — can you find out if the guv'nor is on his way?'

'Righto.' I used my 'talking brooch' for this call. My *bat-phone* (personal radio) has a radio microphone or talking brooch, as we call it. It's space-age equipment. The mike is neatly clipped onto my epaulette, and the battery pack is enclosed in its harness. I see that Ruff stuffed the body of *his* personal radio into a bulging rear trouser pocket and clipped his 'brooch' to his belt. He didn't bother to use the harness at all. That's against 'bat phone' guidelines. Nevertheless, his chosen method of carrying bulky equipment seemed very practicable. I made a mental note I would copy his idea in future.

I made the call. 'Quebec Mike One, Quebec Mike One from Seven Six. Are you receiving?'

There was no answer. 'Quebec Mike One?' I asked again. I heard an assortment of plunking and pinging noises — as if someone played a Jew's harp near the transmitter. There was no response from the duty officer.

'Probably having a shit,' Ruff said.

'I know how he feels,' I replied as I broke wind again. This time it was silent but deadly.

'Quebec Mike? Are you receiving?' I failed to raise the duty officer, so I called the station.

'Go ahead, Sarge.'

'Do you know if the duty officer is on his way to the High Street for the bridge jumper?'

'The guv'nor is informed. I don't know if he's on his way.'

'Noted.'

After that, Ruff led the way toward a muddy slope that would take us onto the railway track. I noticed he managed to avoid plentiful turds and brambles. Though his boots slipped on a layer of foul sludge. I followed Ruff up the steep incline. Thorns snagged my clean tunic. Nettles rustled against my legs, and they rasped against my well-pressed trousers. The rain turned bitter yellow as blobs flicked me in the eye. Inches before I reached the top of the slope, my left boot came into direct contact with a patch of foul-smelling, creamy slime. Unfortunately, I had put all my weight onto *that* foot. My knees buckled under me, and I began to slide down the slope on my backside. During this long, helpless slip, my tunic became spattered with muck and sewage. On the way down my freshly pressed uniform trousers got torn by green bottle-glass. 'Holy shit,' I growled.

By then, Ruff Palmerston had reached the top of the bank. He shouted down, 'What is taking you so long, Skipper?'

I pulled myself to my feet. Then immediately slipped on more dog-mess and went arse-over-tit. 'Bollocks,' I growled.

After that — bit by bit — I made my way *back* to the top edge of the rail embankment to join Constable Palmerston.

Ruff examined me. He saw the mud and excrement all over my uniform and indicated I should turn around so that he might examine the rear of my uniform trousers. He told me they were torn and had a full patch of squelchy stuff — something like diarrhoea — spread across the buttock area.

'Join the fucking professionals,' Ruff said.

'Exactly.'

From our position, at the top of the slope, Ruff and I could see the male jumper. He stood in the distance, positioned on the edge of the wall. He gazed down into the street. Even though the rain had strengthened, we could see that the man was of Indian extraction.

I walked close to Ruff as we made our way, with caution, along the uneven verge beside the rail-track. Once we got to some sooty brickwork that formed a parapet, Ruff stopped.

'I do not want the geezer frightened by my radio. So, I will make calls now — then I'll pull my battery out. You wait here — but be prepared to rush him if I shout,' Ruff explained.

I nodded agreement.

'Quebec Mike from four-one-three.'

'Go ahead, Ruff.'

'Yeah. I am up on the bridge. With the new Skipper. I can see the male jumper. RC4. About five-eight. Approx. forty years old. Received?'

'Yeah, got that.'

'Do you have anything on him?'

'Yes, the description corresponds with Mister Achyuta Patel. His daughter reported the geezer missing last night. He was supposed to get home from his warehouse about seven. He often goes to the pub for a few sherbets after work. They left it till midnight before they reported him missing. Somebody gave his old lady a rattle an hour ago, and she says he hasn't arrived home yet. So best guess is that Patel is your man on the bridge.'

'What's his address?'

'Three One One Viscount Avenue. Near your location.'

'Received.'

Ruff unclipped the battery-pack from his radio and stuffed it into his tunic pocket.

'Righto skip,' he explained, 'I will not be in radio contact for a few minutes. If I need you — I will scream. Or wave like a madman. Got that?'

'Yes.'

'Wait here.'

7

Ruff edged his way along the bridge, to get closer to the jumper. When twenty feet away, the Indian man turned his head. 'Don't make me do it —' he yelled.

Ruff held up both his hands — like a Vegas magician — to show he had nothing to hide. 'Whatever you say, boss.' Although he edged a bit closer.

'I said, don't make me do it —' repeated the man. I observed, at that stage, that the Indian man held a small object in his right hand. I could not reliably describe the article from my distance. I did not have a clear view.

'I will bloody do it. I really will,' yelled the man.

I heard a cracking sound. As if the man snapped his fingers.

'I can't help you if I don't know what you are doing —' Ruff said. 'What are you bloody clicking?'

'My lighter, isn't it? My bloody bleeding cigarette lighter. I am covered in gas. I am going to light up.'

'Need a light? Can I get you a light?' asked Ruff.

'No bloody lights. No bloody lights.' The man seemed extra-irritated by that suggestion. He faltered on the ledge.

'I'm sorry, chum —' said Ruff. 'No lights. No lights. Calm down. Calm down.'

The man began to laugh insincerely. Empty laughter that meant nothing.

'What's going on Mister Patel?' Ruff asked, with good-natured patience.

'It's bloody over, isn't it? I bloody end it. Aren't I? I am going to sacrifice myself. Isn't it?'

'Sacrifice yourself?'

'Yes — I doused myself with gas. I will brighten up your day. I will put on a fiery spectacle. I will show them damn bastards down there. I will put on a bloody good show for them.'

'I ache for you. I really do, Mr. Patel,' Ruff said. 'I want to be with you for a while — I want to be your friend — but I have got to do something first. Do you mind if I step away and do something? I will come back. I promise.'

'You can do what you bleeding like. Isn't it?'

'Yes. But I want your permission first. Do you mind if I step away?'

The man shrugged.

'Thank you, Mr. Patel. I will come right back to you.'

8

Ruff cut back to where I stood. I had backed off a little; now I was about thirty paces from the man on the bridge. When Ruff reached me, he grabbed the battery from his pocket and slapped it back into his bat-phone. 'Quebec Mike One from four-one-three. Are you receiving?' Ruff called the Inspector.

'Go ahead, four-one-three.'

'Yes, Guv. Are you with the Fire Brigade yet?'

'Affirmative four-one-three. What is the situation up there?'

'Guv. Can you get me one — I repeat, one — fireman to bring up a fire blanket and a dry powder extinguisher. Bring to this position, received? Confirm you received?'

'R5 four-one-three. All received. What is the current state of play on the bridge?'

'Get the fireman to maintain contact with the new skipper. He will be at the top of the railway embankment. Near where we parked the station van. The skipper will meet the fireman at the top of the bank. Do you receive?'

'Yes, all received four-one-three. What are the circumstances on the bridge?'

'Thanks, Guv. I'll be out of radio contact for the next few minutes.

Will you get the fire-blanket and extinguisher up here on the hurry-up?' With that, Ruff took his radio battery out again.

'Did you get all that?' he asked.

I nodded.

'Great. Go back to the muddy slope and wait for the fireman to arrive. Once you've got the fire-blanket and extinguisher in your *Germans*, come straight back here. Don't run. Walk briskly. Do not bring anyone else with you. Particularly don't bring back that fucking idiot Inspector Beedi.'

Once I had retrieved the fire blanket, and extinguisher, like Ruff told me, I made my way back as instructed. By now, Ruff had inched closer towards the man on the bridge. I guessed they were approximately eight paces apart. The wind changed direction. I detected the odour of petrol fumes in the air. Ruff stood with his arms stretched and his open palms facing the male RC4.

'Mr. Patel, you have money problems?' he asked. I moved forward two steps to try to hear their conversation.

'Yes, the bloody money troubles is all around me. My girl, she will marry. But do I have enough for wedding? No, I do not. My stock is failing. Now my uncle wants his money back. He yells at me this and he screams at me that. He says I am bloody gambling. I had some flutters. That is true. Now he says, 'Give me my bloody cash back.' And with that, I lose everything. The warehouse, my home, my daughter. Even my wife. She says to me: 'Why do you drink? Why are you always in bloody pub?' I tell her, 'You do not understand, woman. I have money problems.' She says, 'You are cursed.' Bloody right. I know I'm cursed.'

'But this is not the way, buttercup. Honestly, it isn't,' Ruff said. He tried his best to calm the man down.

'Yes, it's the hardest way I am sure...' replied the man on the bridge. 'But I am cursed, anyway. So, who cares?'

'Think about it Mr. Patel. The nice insurance people will not pay out if you do yourself in.' Ruff paused to let the fact sink into the man's befuddled brain. 'Your daughter would rather have you alive for her wedding, wouldn't she? I know that...'

I heard the clicking sound again. Mr. Patel flicked at his petrol lighter. Ruff needed to think fast.

'Your wife will see sense, mind she does. You are a good-looking lad. She will weep when you are gone. Your wife will be sad. You have been a strong partner. Your uncle will be cut-up too... when you are not around to run the storehouse.'

The flicking stopped.

'Your daughter is very beautiful,' Ruff added.

'You have seen her?' asked the man.

'Yeah, sure,' lied Ruff. 'I went over to Viscount Avenue. Before I came to chat with you.'

'Was she crying?'

'Yes, she is terribly upset. So is your missus. They said they can get things sorted out. They said they talked with your uncle. They got him to see sense.'

'They did?'

I noticed these comments had temporarily diverted the man's attention. He seemed interested in what Ruff was telling him.

'Do you mind if I step away again Mr. Patel? I will come right back.' This time the Indian man did not argue. He nodded agreement.

Ruff edged back to my position and grabbed the fire blanket. He unpacked it from its rubberized cover, then folded the blanket like a triangle so it resembled a shawl. He put the thick triangle of wool around his shoulders, over his tunic. Then slipped the extinguisher inside, so it could not be seen. After that, he pulled the makeshift 'shawl' around his neck.

'Brrr!' he told me. 'It's fucking cold up here.'

I regarded Ruff with a doubtful stare. I felt exasperated because I thought, at the stage, he had asked me to bring the blanket over for *him*. I didn't know he had a plan.

9

Ruff returned to the man on the bridge. This time he got within five paces.

'Hello, Mr. Patel. My colleague, down there, he chatted with your wife. I think we can help.'

'You can?'

'Yes, we have special police fund you see. We have money set aside for unexpected events like these.'

Ruff waited. The man seemed interested.

'You may have a fund...' said the man, 'But you will not pay off my gambling debts, will you?' He was clearly in a cycle of despair.

'Yes, actually we *will* payout. That's what the police fund is intended for.'

'Is it?'

The man gawked down from the bridge and into the street. He glanced at the empty petrol can that had been left by the lip of the bridge.

'Brrr!' said Ruff. 'It's harry taters up here, isn't it?' And with these words, the Constable pulled the blanket 'shawl' around his neck and shoulders. He smiled to suggest it might be warm *inside*.

'It is very bloody cold up here...' said the Indian man, 'I cannot hold out much longer. My legs are bloody going numb.' He stared with envy at Ruff's blanket. 'The gasoline — it dripped onto my knees. My shins are getting bloody frozen by it.'

'You will need to hold on a bit longer old lad,' Ruff told him. 'But I can let you wear this if you want to. It's warm, wrapped up in this. Do you want to wear it? I don't mind sharing. It's nice. We can chat about the police fund once you've put it on. Also, we will chat about your daughter's wedding. I had a thought about the wedding. Do you think you might invite someone like me?'

The man suddenly became interested in that concept. He stepped away from the bridge-wall and moved towards Ruff. As he moved, he said, 'Do you want to come to my daughter's marriage? A British officer honouring my family? That would be a true blessing.'

'I would be most privileged to attend your wedding. Can I expect an invitation?' The man's knees shook uncontrollably. His lower jaw chattered. I could see, even from my position, that the man's eyes were bloodshot.

Ruff removed the fire-blanket from around his shoulders. He smiled at the man with renewed optimism. At the same time, I detected that he discreetly dropped the fire extinguisher to his feet. Ruff reached out and handed the blanket to Mr. Patel. It appeared a very heavy item. He urged Mr. Patel to get closer and take it. It looked like it was difficult to hold onto the blanket with an over-stretched arm. 'You will have to come and fucking get it. If you really want it...' I heard the officer mutter — loud enough for me to hear — so I imagine the man heard the words too. 'You need to get close old chap...' Ruff said in voice of authority. 'Put the shawl around your shoulders. Keep warm.'

The man shuffled closer.

It was over in a jiffy.

Ruff snatched back the proffered blanket. Then flicked it out again — this time like a tablecloth. He threw the largest and weightiest part of the blanket directly onto Mr. Patel's head. The sheer heft of the blanket, and the swiftness of the action, caught the man by surprise. The burden of the fire blanket sent him tumbling to the ground, clear of the perilous drop. The Indian man fell onto the relative safety of the cinders.

Once Mr. Patel had been grounded Ruff shouted 'Hey.'

I ran forwards to help. Ruff scrambled to pinpoint the cigarette lighter that had been dropped in the commotion. He couldn't find it. So, Ruff rose to his feet. 'I'm sorry about this old chap —' he told the jumper. Ruff pulled the blanket from the man's chilled body and bent his knees to locate the dry powder extinguisher dropped by his boots. He took hold of the device, pulled out the pin, then lifted the cylinder. Ruff directed the nozzle at the prone man's legs. He gave a ten-second burst of dust. He made sure the man's trousers and waist band were saturated. Once those areas were drizzled with powder, he plastered the rest of the body with what remained. Mr. Patel had been completely overwhelmed. Ruff wrapped him tightly in the fire-blanket.

Then the Constable then lifted the man's body — like a rag-doll — and began to make his way from the dangerous bridge.

'You OK? Do you want help?' I asked.

'I'm fine. As long as you do not light-up, cock. Do you smoke by the way? I forgot to ask.'

'No, as a matter of fact I do not,' I said.

'Good. Can you get on the bat phone again, Skipper? Ask for an ambulance to bring up a hospital stretcher or wheelchair. Something that this prat can be tied onto. Then we can get him down that slippery hill safely. And tell everyone — repeat it twice — 'No Smoking' until this thing is over. That is vital. Nobody is to smoke. Got it? Also, contact Quebec Mike One and tell him to meet us near the van so we can get this crazy sectioned under the Mental Health Act.'

I made the necessary radio call.

The duty Inspector called back. He wanted to speak to Ruff. 'Tell the guv'nor that my hands are full. I cannot talk now.'

I passed on the message.

'Also tell him to stop fucking disturbing me —' Ruff added. 'Especially when I'm trying to do my fucking job.'

10

Once the incident on the bridge had been appropriately completed — and Mr. Patel had been taken off to the local Mental Hospital at Shenley — the relief reassembled back at Quebec Mike for a well-earned cup of *Rosy Lee*.

At the station, I met a man I now know to be Inspector Clifford Beedi.

Mr. Beedi was the duty officer on that first morning of my shift and my new supervising Inspector. He caught hold of me and led me towards his office for what he described as a 'quick chat.' Beedi invited me to take a seat, then slammed the door shut.

'Welcome to Quebec Mike,' he muttered. 'I'm glad you're here. We need a young Sergeant willing to take charge.'

'Nice to be here,' I replied.

'How do you suppose things went on the Bridge?'

'Alright, I think.' I glanced at my mud-stained attire. I looked a proper mess. 'I have never been to a jumper before. Constable Palmerston helped me,' I told him.

'Yes. I wanted to talk about that. I would have preferred it if you had a commanding role in the incident.' I felt annoyed by the suggestion. So, I shifted my leg and bit my top lip.

'Well, I was on the bridge...' I told Beedi. 'I was there in the thick of things.'

'But you *did not* make command decisions, did you?' he growled. 'I hoped you would take a leading role, Sergeant. Still, it does not matter. It's your first day, I suppose. I trust you will do better in the coming days.'

'Everything went smoothly, didn't it?' I asked.

'Not really —' said the Inspector.

'Actually, I thought Constable Palmerston did a wonderful job,' I interrupted. 'I meant to speak to you about putting him up for a commendation, *perhaps* —'

'A commendation? Are you out of your mind? If anything, the officer should be stuck on the dab.'

'Stuck on? What for?'

'He failed to comply with orders. He put everyone in danger. His actions brought the Force into disrepute.'

'Into disrepute?' I asked. My jaw dropped.

'Yes. I spoke to my friend —the Fire Brigade officer on scene. He told me that if Mr. Patel had managed to set himself alight, he would have gone up in a fireball. He says the officers who dealt with the incident were reckless.'

'Reckless?'

'Yes. He told me it was a hazardous situation up there. Just one tiny spark from Patel's lighter would have ignited the petrol. Of course, the jumper would have died in an instant. He'd be the lucky one. You and Palmerston would have been caught in a vacuum. A void that would have killed you both before the ensuing inferno. You would have been brown bread long before you got burned. Suffocated, you see. It would have been a painful way to go, he says. There was no one up there to save you. You should've had the boys from the Brigade on that bridge. The ambulance lads too. And you should have asked for specialist back-up.'

'Specialist back-up?'

'Yes. The Fire Brigade officer said the madman should have been dealt with uncompromisingly. They suggest he should have been shot. From a distance. We should have called for a marksman. That's the only safe way to deal with an idiot who douses himself with gasoline and seems intent on flaming himself. You should *not* have been unduly influenced by Constable Palmerston. You were both mindless. I have a good mind to issue pocketbook warnings to you both. For reckless behaviour.'

At that stage, I thought it wise to explain my role on the bridge: 'As I said, Constable Palmerston did all the talking. He made sure I was kept at a safe distance from the man with the petrol. I didn't get close. I think Ruff handled the risk well. And he saved the man's life, didn't he? Isn't that worthy of appreciation?'

'Well, I would have preferred it if the man had been *shot*. I certainly would have preferred it if I had made the command decisions. Or, perhaps, if *you* had directed things better and included me in the decision-making process. Time after time, I asked for a report from the Bridge — neither of you updated me. Is that how you do things in the West End?'

'No, sir. I ought to have kept you informed. I'm sorry.'

'Good. We'll leave it at that. But I do not want your judgement to become influenced by Constable Palmerston in the future. Is that clear?'

'Yes, sir.'

'And it is precisely on the subject of Constable Palmerston that I want to see you today. He's the subject of a long enquiry that I have set-up into his conduct and discipline. I want you to study him closely over the coming weeks. I want you to compile a dossier.'

'A dossier?'

'Yes. Note each time that he fails to comply with your orders. Discover his little scams and record them. And uncover his bad habits. Also, make notes of his blunders. Document his snide comments. Get the dirt on this Ruff Palmerston. I want to get a file together for A10 complaints. As you know, the Commissioner wants all the bad-eggs thrown out.'

'Is Constable Palmerston a bad egg? He seems popular with the lads.'

'Of course, he's a bad egg. You've seen the evidence, *already* haven't you? You will find he is devious and resourceful. He requires close supervision. It's why I'm assigning you to keep an eye on him. Make sure you observe him with all diligence. And compile that dossier.'

'Yes, sir.'

Someone knocked at the Inspector's door.

'Enter' Beedi boomed, just like the headmaster at my old school. I walked an ancient-looking sergeant. This grizzled Skipper had a broad smile, rubicund face, and a sprinkling of white hair.

'Hello, Paddy' Inspector Beedi said, as he welcomed the Sergeant.

'Good morning, sir,' The old lad said. He tumbled his ancient bones into a soft chair by the window. He was out of breath.

'This is our new Skipper. Clarence Chesterfield.' The Inspector said.

The old man raised his bum, momentarily, to shake my hand, then collapsed with a giant puff. Once settled, he said: 'Nice to meet you.'

'Paddy Gallaher is our most experienced Skipper here at Quebec Mike' the Inspector explained. 'He's up for retirement shortly. Aren't you Paddy?'

'Six months to go, sir.'

'Paddy is my right-hand man. He helps around the station. He deals with the office. Looks after books. Keeps things clean and tidy. He oversees communications and does his part in the Charge Room. Don't you Paddy?'

'Yes, sir.'

'In other words, Paddy doesn't go on the streets anymore. That's why I need a young Section Sergeant to help me. It's why I asked for you. I require you to supervise all the incidents, complete daily taskings and, in general, keep all the men in check. Can you handle that?'

'Yes sir,' I told him.

'Good. I want you to take daily parades. Do the duty roster. Assign officers to patrols and supervise incidents. Of course, you will be expected to do a few stints in the Charge Room. But, overall, I want you to focus on working with the lads on the section. Out on the streets. Got that?'

'Yup.'

'Very well. I'm sure we'll get along fine. You'll see we have a good team here. I want you to meet everybody as soon as you can. Work with *all* the team-members and study their little ways. But, as I already said, pay close attention to Palmerston. He seems to think he controls this relief. And he does not. See you remind him of that. Often. Ram home the point if you must...' At this stage, the Inspector made a fist with his right hand and winked at the old Sergeant as he punched the desk. The Sergeant nodded his agreement. 'Palmerston must remember he works for me. It's not the other way around. If you need to knock that fact into him, I shan't get involved...'

'Very well, sir.'

'Well, that's it. Don't forget, all I told you.'

Paddy and I were waved from the Inspector's office.

'We'll grab some Rosy,' Suggested Paddy. He lit a stubby cigar. 'Don't mind Beedi too much. I know he's an old lady — but his heart is in the right place.'

'He gave me a proper bollocking about this morning's jumper,' I said, as Paddy blew a thick shroud of smoke my way. 'He thought we were in grave danger on the bridge.'

'Well, that's because you allowed Ruff to get *above himself*. The Inspector has something against Ruff. They detest one another. The boss wants to be shot of him.'

'He told me to compile a dossier.'

'He asked me to do that too. I didn't get around to it.'

'I see.'

'But you will *have to* do it won't you son?'

'Will I?'

'Yes, you will. Because you are a probationary Sergeant, lad. Beedi has the power to send you back to C Division. From whence you came. Back to street-toms, shoplifters, and drunks. You had better impress him. Or you won't be confirmed in the rank.'

'I see,' I whispered.

11

I went into the canteen for tea and toast.

The lads on the relief had pulled two mess-tables together and were seated around it. They played cards — knock-out whist.

Predictably, Constable Ruff Palmerston took his position at the head of the table. His tunic was undone, his tie loosened. A trusty pack of Benson & Hedges by his side. He had stuck a playing card onto his forehead with spit. Presumably, this would be the next card he placed. 'If you like cheese — you'll fucking hate these,' he announced in his peculiar, singsong style. I assume his accent originated in the Black Country.

'Don't get overly confident, whippie-whappie,' said Godfrey Lambert. 'I have one here that will give your trumping a bumping.' With a satisfied smile, the older man threw down a Jack. After that, he took a contented drag on his pipe.

'You grunty faced old shit-bag' said another Constable. This Constable looked about twenty years old. I now know him to be Peter Prince. Or Peter 'the Ponce' Prince as he's known by his colleagues. Peter Prince flicked a ten of hearts onto the table. The highest trump in his hand. Manifestly he was the 'baby' of the relief. Thin as a rake, he had a mad thicket of collar-length 'toddler's hair' and a fresh round face that seemed to shout, 'I'm eager to please.' The young

Constable pushed back his chair with an air of submission and declared he was about to fetch the tea.

'Milky coffee for me, Ponce —' Ruff Palmerston said, without taking his eyes from the hand.

'Me too,' muttered Godfrey.

'What a bunch of tossers,' Peter Prince sighed. He spied me standing near: 'What about you Skip? Can I get you a drink?'

I ordered tea and joined Peter Prince at the canteen counter. A large West Indian lady shuffled over at the speed of a smashed slug. 'What you want, honey?' she whispered, with a frown.

Constable Prince ordered teas and coffees plus a chocolate biscuit for himself. 'And give me a little of your loving sweetness too...' he added. The catering assistant returned a disdainful glower as if he was the pissiest-assed vagrant she had ever seen, while she was the Queen of fucking Sheba.

'Do I have to put up with this Sarge?' she asked before she sucked in her teeth. I meant to offer an apology of sorts, but we heard a cry from the card table: 'Eye's up —' someone shouted. 'There's fanny in the house...' All the lads put their playing cards on the surface to gaze at two fancy-ladies who strolled through the canteen entrance.

These birds were dolled up to the nines and looked bloody marvellous. 'C.I.D typists,' Peter Prince whispered. 'The dark-haired one is screwing the D.I. for your info. The S.P on the other is she's on the rebound. You might get lucky with her. Fancy your chances?'

The girls tottered over to the counter. The fair-haired dolly gave me the once over, and I smelt Lux soap on her skin and mint imperials on her breath. The dark-haired tart blanked me.

'Can I get a drink for you girls? Tea or coffee?' I offered.

The dark-haired one brushed me aside with the practised ease of an expert: 'No thank you,' she pronounced, without even looking in my direction. She turned to the catering manager, and smiled: 'Hello Daloris, two tea and two toast love when you're good and ready....'

'Coming right up,' said the black lady. She ignored the priority of us police officers, even though we'd been in line before the birds.

'Blimey! That's charming that is...' Peter Prince said. 'Slappers in knickers get preference over boys in blue.'

'Same the world over,' I told him, with a philosophical nod and a slap to his shoulder.

As we waited, I examined the canteen. The lads had gone back to their card game. But every now-and-then one would peep over his cards to leer at the fancy birds by the counter.

'I get a lazy-lob standing near them,' sighed Constable Prince, nodding to the typists again. I chose to ignore his comment. Two members of the relief sat on their own, separated from the others. 'Why are they not sitting with the rest?' I asked. Constable Prince glanced to where I gazed. 'They don't play cards. Or rather they've been fleeced too often by Ruff.'

'I see.'

'The guy with the glasses is 'Smart' Wally West. He's been in the Job five years. They call him 'Smart' because *he's not*. The other one — the one reading the book — is Martin Duke. Martin is dull as ditchwater. Everybody calls him Fart'n Mart'n — because everything he does ends up smelling of shit. He's been in the job six years and is cramming for promotion. The guv'nor thinks the sun shines out of his weedy arse. He's the boss's man.'

'I saw him already, nearly run-me-the-fuck over in his Panda this morning.'

Eventually, our beverages arrived. I raised my cup to Constable Peter Prince — to indicate thanks —then strolled to the card game.

'Want to deal?' asked Ruff. He handed me the deck.

I shuffled and cut the pack, quickly and proficiently. I dealt the cards around the table and turned over the topmost card.

'Spades are trumps' all the lads said in unison.

'Game fucking on....' I declared.

12

The Score and the Lah-Di-Dah

The next morning, I joined Constable Ruff Palmerston on the station van. I asked Constable 'Misty' Bill Winfield to accompany us. Winfield was a spotty Constable who moaned— more than once — that he had completed a Panda course. He felt irritated that I took him off the Panda posting to put him on the van with Ruff. I did it deliberately because I had seen nothing of him the preceding day. I wanted to learn about *all* the different characters on my new relief and that included 'Misty' Bill who had been mysteriously vacant during the Bridge Jumper incident.

Bill sat huffily in the van, by Ruff, so I squeezed by his side, in front.

Our first call of the day was to a mother who had found a 'stock of pornography' hidden under her son's bed. She kept the lad off school and had phoned the police. We went to Myrtle Grove where we parked outside a clean bungalow that had clean net curtains and a regimental line of well-pruned roses that led to a front porch. The three of us went to the entrance and 'Misty' Bill rung the bell. A woman aged about fifty opened the door. She wore a blue-plastic housecoat and a pair of yellow Marigold's. She pulled the rubber gloves off with a spur-of-the-moment crack.

'Good morning —' She beckoned us in with a thin smile. We removed our helmets and entered the well-ordered hallway. 'It is about my son, officers. The dirty little sod. He hid a stack of dirty magazines under his bed. I thought you better be informed. I found the trove of smut this morning when I hoovered out his room.'

'What? Did you call the police for this?' Misty protested.

'Button it...' Ruff hissed, under his breath.

The woman took us to the boy's bedroom.

In a tiny room sat a teenager with eyes reddened by recent tears. He sat on a candlewick bedspread and wore a smart 'private school' uniform. He offered us a bitter smile as we traipsed into his private space.

'Here —' the woman said. She reached under the bed and pulled out a pile of girlie mags. Knave, Whitehouse, Park Lane, Fiesta and Parade. We took the skin-rags from her and flicked through them. There wasn't much in them — nothing you might call obscene. Merely a young boy's collection of titties and fluff.

'Ashamed of yourself now?' the mother asked her son. He shifted his feet and gave a shame-faced stare.

'Does the lad have any drugs 'n' shit — or something serious?' Misty asked. 'Only this shit is just petty...'

The woman grimaced at the word 'shit.' She'd never heard such dirty language in her Christian home before. 'Isn't this obscenity enough?' she declared, before adding, 'He should be put away.'

I examined one of the raunchiest mags in the collection. I stopped at the centrefold — it featured a blond tart who held her Jack and Danny open. A well-placed banana pointed at the velvety muff.

'OK love,' Ruff said 'We'll take it from here — we will take a look around. Then we'll talk to your son. Put the kettle on. We will join you for a cuppa in a few minutes.' The lady seemed irritated when she heard this but went away to fix the tea anyhow. Ruff pushed the bedroom door shut with his size fourteen boot.

'Right lad. Do you have any other shit? How about drugs or weapons? Anything we might be interested in?' The boy shook his head. 'Mind if we look around?' We started to search the room anyway — without waiting for an answer. Ruff got the boy to stand, to examine under the mattress.

Meanwhile I searched behind the wardrobe. Misty pulled out his drawers one-by-one so he could get his hand behind the rear of the unit. Nothing could be found.

'What's your favourite one son?' asked Ruff. He shuffled the stack of magazines in front of the lad's eyes as if they were oversized playing cards. The boy did not know whether to answer or not. 'Come on, son. I haven't got all bleeding day. Which one is best?' The youth indicated the magazine I held between my fingers. The one with the gaping fanny.

'Do me a favour and don't let your mother find it again. Right?' Ruff said with a wink. He pulled the glossy magazine from my hands and passed it to the boy. 'Hide it well. In a better place, this time. We will have to confiscate the others though. Otherwise, your mother will think we're not doing our job. OK?' The boy nodded.

———

Back in the lounge, we sat on lace-covered wing chairs and sipped tea. The woman used her best china set to impress us. Ruff had placed the stack of grumble-mags by his huge black boots. 'We will be taking these dirty mags with us, ma'am,' he explained. 'As you know — this type of literature is not on sale to minors. We need to investigate where your son got hold of them.'

The woman tutted. 'Yes. It's all quite disgusting. You will take my son in for questioning, I suppose?'

'Well the thing is...' continued Ruff. 'Your son is a *victim* here. Not a suspect —'

The woman seemed surprised to hear it. 'How so?' she enquired.

Ruff explained, 'He's only a lad. With natural urges, normal impulses, and customary needs. He must hate being shut up like a prisoner in this fucking nursing home. It must be a living hell for the little sod. You ought to give him more leeway. Allow him to live his life. Let him be a regular kid.'

The mother appeared agitated by these comments. Her face went red, and she jumped up, smoothed her housecoat, then collected the bone china. 'You have out-stayed your welcome, officers...' she mumbled. 'I have never heard anything like it in my life. I pay my rates, you know. I expect courtesy from the authorities.'

'Thanks for the tea, ma'am,' Misty said. We struggled to get out of the room any faster. Ruff took the girlie mags with him.

'Well, at least you will be getting rid of those disgusting things' said the woman as she opened the front door. She gave her sourest look to me — because she had seen the fresh white stripes on my arm.

'Yes, these will be destroyed in the incinerator back at our station. Once enquiries have been completed,' Ruff told her.

'Good morning,' she said in conclusion.

'Stupid old bat,' Misty muttered, loud enough for her to hear. We trudged back to the van.

'Do we have an incinerator at the station?' I asked Ruff, in all innocence.

'Of course not,' he said with a grin. 'This little cache will add agreeably to our shit-house collection, though, won't it?'

After refreshments, we took a call from Comms regarding a female wandering. Apparently, she could be found near the Bel Air estate on Montclair Road. Ruff took the station van out to the country. Misty, still grumpy about not being permitted to drive a Panda, opted to stay in the back of the van, on the bench-seat 'for a nap.'

I admit that arriving at an 'outer borough' had been a culture shock for me. For example, I did not realize how bucolic the area around North West London could be. We roared by open spaces, dense thickets — even farms. I didn't know there were farms in the M.P.D. We travelled past a sleepy school that reminded me of St Trinian's —

then we toured along a broad avenue that stretched for miles into a blurred horizon. That's where we spied the old girl. She hobbled along the footpath in muddy bedroom slippers, with her ripped winceyette nightgown and hair-crackers flapping in the wind. Ruff pulled the van onto the weed-strewn footway to halt her progress. The puzzled old dear gazed at us with a gentle and congenial expression on her wrinkled, soft face. I could see a neat row of pearly-white dentures that glinted in the early afternoon sun. Her tight cluster of pure white curls was held in place by strips of material. Her lips were parched, and her eyes sore. Even though she must have been ninety — she had the bearing and grace of a woman who'd been gorgeous all her life.

'Hello, Princess. How are you today?' Ruff asked.

The old booby reminded me of the Queen Mother. She gave Ruff a bright smile. 'Hello young man,' she said, 'Do you know my son? He is a man of the sea.'

'Yes. I know him personally,' Ruff said with a wink. 'He wants to know why you are so far from home...'

'Enos. I'm off to see Enos. I said I'd give him the money.'

'All right, Princess. We can take you to see Enos. Save your walking. How do you want to travel? Upfront with us?'

The old lady seemed unenthusiastic about that idea. 'There is no need to see Enos right now. I am fine walking.'

'But you see — we have been sent to get you. Enos sent us.'

'Oh? Is that right?' She asked. Then she nodded as if she'd made up her mind.

'Squeeze into our van.' Ruff told her. 'My friend will sit next to you. We'll take you to see Enos.'

'Oh. Thank you. That is very thoughtful of you.'

Ruff went to take her hand but stopped when he saw that she clutched a large wodge of paper-bills in her sweaty palms.

'What have you there, princess?' Ruff asked, intrigued.

'It's money. It's for Enos. Three hundred guineas. Like he asked.' She held out her hand to expose the crumpled bundle of twenties.

'Christ,' Ruff said. 'There's three months' pay there.' He folded her hand over the notes.

'Do me a favour, Princess. Deliver the money to my friend with the stripes. He'll look after it better than I can.'

The old lady contemplated me with milky eyes: 'Yes. Of course. He looks a most respectable young man. That is dear of you. You will make sure that Enos gets it, won't you?' I nodded as I grabbed the small fortune.

Ruff helped the dear lady into the van. He pushed her rump up the steps, then slid her body across the bench seat. After she settled, I sat beside. I peeked at the warm *lucre* in my hands. Then I glanced at the wrinkly. She returned a cheery smile.

Ruff called the nick: 'Quebec Mike from four-one-three. Are you receiving?'

'Go ahead, Ruff.'

'We spotted the wandering lady on Montclair Road. Have you any updates your end? '

'Her name is Mabel. According to a step-niece she had been a famous actress in silent films. She walked away from her home on Tambora Crescent six hours ago. Her address is Kaywoodie house.'

'Cheers, Quebec Mike.'

———

We drove to Kaywoodie House. We found a magnificent villa designed in the Tudor style. We crunched along a splendid path, and we viewed a woman aged about forty years who stood at the marble portico. She had a Dalmatian puppy at her feet.

'There you are Aunt,' said the lady as I opened the van door. 'You know you should not go off alone. To wander the streets. Tssk! And you are still wearing your nightgown too.'

'I went to see Enos. He asked for the money you know,' the old lady told her.

'Enos was her first husband.' The step-niece explained. 'Of course, he's been dead thirty years.'

I handed the spotty-dog lady the wodge of twenty-pound notes. 'It's hers....' I said.

'Why did you take all this cash with you, Aunt dear?'

'Enos asked for it.'

'I haven't counted it.' I told the woman. 'I don't even know if it's all there. She may have dropped some cash on her walking expedition. She didn't have a purse with her but had the notes wrapped in her hand.

'Oh, never mind. That's not important. The main thing is that she's back with us. She's safe.'

'Is there anything else we can do?' Ruff asked.

'Look. Do you want to come in for a glass of sherry or something stronger? My way of saying thanks.'

Ruff gazed at me for inspiration, then shook his head. 'I do not think so missus,' he replied, 'But thanks for the thought.'

'Can I offer you something for your time and effort?' The woman rolled out one of the damp a twenty-pound notes and held it under my nose.

'It's so kind of you. I'm sure. But we cannot take it. Thanks again.' We turned around and pounded the gravel back to our van.

'Don't you want the reward?' The lady called.

'Flee for your life. Do not look behind, Sarge,' Ruff told me. 'Lest we both be swept away by cruel temptation.'

13

The Anthony Blunt

On the return trip from the 'The Wandering Lah-Di-Dah,' Ruff attempted to pull a wallet from his trouser-pocket — a difficult task to achieve in safety because he hammered down the country road like a furious rally-driver making up time. He managed the awkward arrangement by holding the steering wheel between his chunky knees while he fumbled with his pocket, both hands off the wheel.

'Me and my lady went to Majorca for our holidays last year,' he proclaimed. He pronounced the island as 'Marr-Jorkaa.'

'My old lady couldn't wait to get her knockers out. I think she got randy. What with all the Sangria and the Diego waiters and what-not. Anyhow, she told me she felt free and uninhibited. So, couldn't wait to get her Bristol's out for all to see.'

I oinked a reply but wondered where this story was headed.

Ruff managed to finger open his wallet —though he motored along the highway at 55 mph. It seemed apparent he had no control over the police van. 'So, do you wanna see a picture of my wife topless or not, Skipper?' With the question, he handed over a grimy looking

Polaroid. He placed the photo in my hands, glossy-side down — with the white surface uppermost.

I flipped the picture over. It showed the bare feet of a lady. She stood on the sand. The photo portrayed the lower half of her blue maxi dress. But the top half of the picture had been rudely cropped-off waist height. Chopped in half. What a bastard.

I sneaked a glance at Ruff. His eyes bounced with mischief, and a stupid smirk lingered on his chubby cheeks. At that instant, he reminded me of an overgrown choirboy. 'You got me, Ruff!' I porky-pied. I exaggerated a laugh to show how much I 'appreciated' his little joke. I handed the well-worn Polaroid back to Ruff, and he fingered it back into his wallet. 'Seriously, though, mate — I assume you are *actually* married?'

'Yes. Me and the missus tied the knot before coming down South. My school sweetheart she was. What about you?'

'No. I live at Trenchard. The Section House for single men. I have not found the right woman.'

'Not Ginger Beer, are you?' Ruff dared ask.

'No!' I announced. Giving the refusal an unnecessarily loud ring of protest.

'I only wondered. I thought they were all as bent as nine-bob notes down at Trenchard.'

'Not everyone.' I muttered.

'You should get yourself over to Square Twenty-eight. They have some bints over there. Classy ones too, by all account. Filling the Section House up with Jack and Danny, so they are. Started to put them in about a year ago. The bints are parked on the top floor.'

'Bints?' I asked.

'Yes. Plonks. Square Twenty-eight is going to be full of plonks eventually, so I heard. You should get yourself a section house transfer out of Trenchard and into the plonk-house. Take advantage of all that bintage that's going to waste...' We rushed down the road a couple more miles while Ruff lit a fresh B&H ciggie and allowed the smoke to swirl through a crack in the window. 'Tell you what ...' he said suddenly, 'Why don't you check-yourself-in this Saturday night?

Have a Dicky Bird with the Section House Sergeant. See if he can magic-up a room up for you at Square 28. See if you like the place.'

'Uh-huh.'

'Then come over to our place for a meal after. Meet the trouble and strife. Have grub, grab a drink. Afterwards, get your head down at Square Twenty-eight. You might even meet some of the bints I mentioned. That would be good for you, yeah?'

'It's kind of you to offer, Ruff. Ta very much.'

14

The next morning, I met Ruff's best mate, Constable Dave Yale.

Dave told me he had been off visiting his folks 'up North' for a week. Dave possessed a thin beard, watery-blue eyes, and an arrogant smile. His grin seemed fixed across his mush like a permanent grizzle. Dave remained Ruff's most dependable friend. The two lads shared a special bond and were eager to catch up. I left them to chat in the canteen while I watched the early brew steam. After a while, I strolled out into the fresh morning air. That's where I located Constable Wally West. He prepared our solitary Morris Minor. He said he was taking 'her' out on patrol. It seemed that just one Moggy remained in our fleet. The lads were so fond of this little run-around that they took extra care of her. They maintained the engine, provided her motor with oil, and even wiped down her seats. They did not want this little honey to be taken away by B department and replaced by the square wheeled monstrosity known as the *Aggro* — a.k.a. the ubiquitous Austin Allegro.

'How come you never drive the van, Wally?'

'I'm class five Skipper. Like most of the relief. The only van drivers on our team are Ruff and Dave Yale. And Godfrey Lambert too, of course, since he's Class One. But he's always driving *the car*. Anyway, Ruff likes to drive the van. It's his preferred choice.'

'Why?'

'He likes to make tea. Do the chores.'

'Do you wanna be a van driver?'

'Yes, I would love it. But the guv'nor is determined to get Fart'n Mart'n trained-up next on the van. He thinks Fart'n should become the relief area-car driver when Godfrey Lambert retires....'

'So, Godfrey Lambert is the only Advanced Driver on the team?'

'Yes, Godders did his class-one back in the Sixties. We need *another* top-class driver.'

Equipped with this information, I returned to the canteen to see how the tea had progressed. It hadn't. Instead, I found I'd interrupted a private discussion between Ruff and Dave. They were partaking of a discreet tête-à-tête by the kettle.

'Maybe you should drive the van for us today,' I suggested to Constable Yale.

'Very well, Skipper,' Dave Yale replied.

Ruff gave a dubious look. As if he'd been rumbled. 'What do you want me to do then, Skip?' He asked.

'You can take a Panda out,' I replied. 'I will come along.'

He nodded, then provided me with his best smile.

15

Ruff and I rode out of the yard in one of the blue and white Austin 1100s. As we left the nick, we heard chitter-chatter on the P.R. Ruff clipped the talking brooch to the tobacco-stained sun-visor. The radio call came from Fart'n Mart'n: 'Quebec Mike from one-two-zero. C.V.I. check please.'

'Go ahead, one-two-zero.'

'Oscar Lima Alpha. One-four-zero. Lima. Receive?'

'Stand by one-two-zero,' responded the Comms officer.

'Fart'n Mart'n makes himself sound busy —' Ruff said. 'He does a few car checks each morning to ingratiate himself with the Inspector. They think that checks on stationary cars is vital police work.'

'He might come across a stolen vehicle I suppose,' I put forward.

'Yeah. Pigs might fly,' Ruff replied with a sigh.

'Why don't you like Fart'n Mart'n?' I asked.

'Why? Because he's as windy as a morning shit,' Replied Ruff. 'He is a fucking liability.'

16

Fart'n Mart'n created more work for the Comms officer a little later. He requested two more unnecessary vehicle checks on unattended jam-jars. After that, the Comms officer decided to assign him to a little task. To silence him. 'Martin, when you're done with that last vehicle check — please attend Park Drive. Outside the newsagent. Report of a male causing a disturbance.'

'Noted,' replied Fart'n Mart'n. 'Is there any other unit nearer? I'm still dealing with this unattended vehicle...'

'You're the closest. You are assigned,' Comms replied.

'I suppose we'd better make our way,' Ruff said.

'Do you want me to offer-up for the call?' I asked.

'No. Let Fart'n Mart'n stew. We will let him get there first.'

17

It took about five minutes to get to Park Drive. As we turned into the street, I saw Wally West, in his Moggy Minor, zooming in the opposite direction.

'Where the fuck is he going?' I grumbled. 'That's the *wrong* way — isn't it?'

'Lazy twat,' replied Ruff. 'Another windy asshole. Wally will do anything to avoid confrontation.'

We arrived at the newsagents in Park Drive. As we pulled in, I identified Fart'n Mart'n. He chatted with an intoxicated man who supported himself against a wall while he smoked a fag. Martin stood with his hands in his pockets and his cap on the back of his head.

We jumped out of our Panda and made our way towards them.

'Hello, skip,' said Martin. 'The geezer is behaving now. I convinced him to go home to sleep it off. He's had a few jars. But he's good as gold...'

I examined the man. He seemed unsteady on his feet, and his eyes were glazed. He gawked at me with an air of ugly intent.

'I thought the original call said something about a disturbance?' I suggested. 'Have you identified the informant?'

'No, I went straight for this guy. I had a nice chat with him. He seems reasonable enough. He told me he's about to go home anyway. No further assistance required. This will be just a notebook entry.'

'I see.'

Ruff stood a few steps behind me. I thought I should ask him to seek out the original informant. But just as I was about to do that, the drunk spoke: 'You can stick it right up your jacksie mate...' He burbled. A slither of green snot dribbled from his nose and headed for his top lip, 'I'll take the lot of yerse on. Ye are a group of turd bandits. Pooves — the whole lot of yerse.'

'What did he say?' intervened Ruff.

'Leave it out, Ruff,' pleaded Fart'n Mart'n. 'The guy was fine before *you* got here. He'll calm down, trust me. Leave him.'

'Yes, you,' continued the drunk. 'I am talking to you carrot cunt. Tell your poove mate to give you a tommy tank. You ugly shit-fucks...'

I turned to Fart'n Mart'n, 'Are you going to let him get away with that? Don't you have enough to take this asshole in?'

'He's fine,' reasoned Fart'n Mart'n, shifting his feet. 'He's just a little worse for wear, trust me. He promised to go home and sleep it off... didn't you chummy?'

'Really?' I said.

Then the pisshead pushed himself off the wall. He slung down his burning cigarette, lowered his nut, then rushed us. As he did this, he started to sing: 'Harry Roberts. Harry Roberts. Foxtrot one-one. Foxtrot one-one. Braybrook. Braybrook. Three nil. Three nil...'

I did not notice him move, but Ruff appeared alongside the drunk. He had relocated at lightning speed. Ruff grabbed one of the drunk's shoulders and put all his body weight onto it. At the same time, he put his boot behind the drunken man's back legs and pulled him to the ground. The man tried to gob into the officer's face, but the flob missed by inches. 'Fuck all of yous. Fuck all of yous.' The drunk sang, in a tuneless fashion. 'Up the Provos. Hooray to the IRA. Stephen Tibble is a fag.'

18

'Call for the van Sarge,' Ruff shouted. I made a hurried call.

Ruff managed to get the drunk into a wristlock on the floor. 'Help me get the son of a bitch on his feet. Or he'll piss all over us.' We shoved the fellow to his feet. Fart'n Mart'n had backed-off by that stage. I struggled to see where the bone-idle shithead had got. He'd vanished. Then I guessed what he'd done. He'd returned to the safety of his police car. I called out: 'We could do with more help here.' But Fart'n Mart'n remained cocooned inside his panda. All the doors and windows were closed. He cocked a deaf 'un.

Quickly enough, the station van arrived. The van mounted the curb and came to a squealed halt. The driver, Dave Yale, jumped out of to approach us. He and Ruff grabbed the man to put him in double hammerlocks. The prisoner got dragged towards the back of the van. I rushed around to open the rear doors for them. Once the double-doors were opened, we slid the man inside. He fell forward onto his face. Ruff sat on his shoulders. I pushed the doors closed while this was going on. Dave and Ruff pulled the man's pants down until they were by his knees, to stop him kicking out. After that, they tied his hands behind his back — using the belt they'd pulled it from his waistband.

'One more thing,' Ruff added. He pulled the man's hankie out of his trouser pocket and crammed it between the drunk's teeth. 'To stuff his stinking mouth,' he added. Then he turned to me: 'Skip. Do you want to do the honours and take my Panda back to the nick? I had better stay with this asshole. I'm nicking him for threatening behaviour by the way.'

I gave Ruff a puzzled look. He caught me off balance with the suggestion. 'I'm not a police driver,' I explained.

'You can drive, though, can't you?' he quizzed.

'Sure, I can. Only... I am not qualified to drive police cars. '

'Permit yourself to drive police cars then. You're a fucking Sergeant, aren't you? Take my Panda back to the yard. The keys are under the visor. As per normal. '

With that, the van screamed off — the rear doors banging.

So, I was left alone. To ferry back the Austin police car. Before I left the scene, I scanned around and noticed that Fart'n Mart'n had gone too. *He's probably doing more checks on unattended vehicle* — I thought.

What an Anthony Blunt.

the Anthony Blunt

As suggested by Constable 'Ruff' Palmerston, I arranged for a one-night stay at SQ28 — that's the single officers' quarters located near Quebec Mike. I found the Section House to be modern, well decorated and cosy. When I checked in with the warden I did not catch a glimpse of the mythical 'bints' — but then again, I didn't venture to their domain, the females were ensconced on the top floor.

At six o'clock, I left my quarters to walk the mile-or-so to Ruff's gaff. I wore smart cavalry-twill slacks and a presentable blue blazer. I arrived at St Julian's Crescent in good time for my evening meal with Ruff and his trouble-and-strife. In the small curve of Job Houses, situated in a long Crescent, I saw a group of saucepan-lids playing soccer on a patch of turd-strewn grass. The game took place beneath a sign that brashly stated: 'No ball games.' A man tinkered with a jacked-up Ford Capri... the engine dripped gloopy engine-oil directly into a drain. I heard Bay City Rollers on Capital Radio, and a voice shouted out: *shut that fucking racket up*. I detected the unmistakable odour of burning of meatballs. I saw a young woman putting washing on a line, oblivious to a bonfire that fumed next door. And I saw a grey-haired dog whimper when it got led to a tree by a snivelling toddler. Yes, St Julian's Crescent is police heaven.

I arrived at Job House number 55. A pink coloured building with a low brick wall. Like all the Met Police married quarters, the home was equipped with a blue door. I knocked, and Ruff Palmerston appeared right away. Ruff seemed in a state of cheerful wooziness — as if scarcely woken. But looked pleased to see me: 'Come inside Sarge,' he offered, with a rosy-faced smile. He led me through to the living room and indicated where I should sit — on an orange coloured couch. I pushed away a pile of fresh laundry to make myself room.

'I had a doze...' he explained. 'I did Early Worm this morning. My ninth shift in a row. The last two shifts were doubles. As you can imagine, I'm cream-fucking-crackered. How is the Section House? Did you check in yet? How do you find it?'

'Good, good.'

'See any Señoritas yet?'

'No, *no*. They must be hiding in their lair. They probably heard I was coming.'

'Never mind. I'm sure you'll get an Aylesbury Duck. Positive thinking...' He prodded his nose with an index finger and winked. We both sniggered as Mrs. Palmerston entered the room. She wore a flower-printed apron — purchased with her Green Shield stamps, no doubt — there was a pair of fluffy purple slippers on her bare feet. She had soft brown hair that had been groomed into a clean wedge. She had remarkably bright eyes. 'This is my trouble, Sarge. Hello dear, this is Sergeant Chesterfield.'

I stood to greet Mrs. Palmerston. I handed her the box of Mackintosh's Week-End assortment that I'd brought along.

'How thoughtful.' She took the chocolates and smiled gently. 'You ought to call me Eve. How do you do? Sergeant... er?'

'Clarence,' I replied, somewhat shyly. We both chuckled. She left to get something from the kitchen. In her absence, Ruff lit a ciggie and pulled the floor-standing ashtray near his seat. I surveyed the room. 'Nice place you've got here, Ruff,' I remarked. The room had been decorated to regular Met Police spec, right down to the poster of the 'Wings of Love' and a variety of pot-plant holders.

'My Missus does her own macramé,' Ruff commented as he saw me judging her rope work.

Eve Palmerston returned with a cheese and pineapple hedgehog. 'Some nibbles,' she explained. 'While we have a chat.' She sat in the opposite armchair, across from me, and bummed a light from Ruff. She lit a Silk Cut. 'So, tell me, love, are you going out with anyone at the moment?'

'Damn it, woman.' Ruff said. 'Give the man a chance! He's just got through the bloody door. Are you trying to fix him up already?'

'He doesn't mind. Do you Clarence? We might as well get to know all about him.'

I shuffled my feet and wriggled my butt on the couch. I gave Eve one of my most reliable smiles: 'No, of course I do not mind. I'm not seeing anyone at the moment. I had an on/off relationship with a girl a while back. Of late, it's been more off than it's been on.' I winked.

'A handsome man like you. It's a wicked waste. She must have taken leave of her senses. To let you go —'

'That's what I thought too,' I agreed.

'Well, I have a few contacts on the estate. If you're interested?'

'Bloody Hell. She's matchmaking now,' grumbled Ruff.

Eve turned to her hubby. 'Only if he's interested, dear. He doesn't have to say *yes*...' she turned back: 'There are some lovely girls on the estate. They're all looking for eligible men. They're lonely during the day because their other halves are on early worm.'

I nodded politely.

'Changing the subject...' Ruff said. 'I guess Inspector Beedi gave you his spiel about bad-eggs in the Met?'

'Oh, God. If you're talking job, I'll go and fix supper.' Eve said. She grabbed a cocktail stick and popped a cheese 'n' pineapple chunk between her glossy lips. Then marched off.

'Yup —' I replied. 'Inspector Beedi gave me *the lecture*.'

'Of course, what he didn't tell you...' Ruff continued, 'Is that if a Constable doesn't have a load of 163's plastered all over his bog wall — then he isn't doing his fucking job properly. It's that simple.'

'Do you have a load of 163's plastered on your bog wall?' I asked.

'Go look. I'm proud of the complaint forms. I've been one-six-three'd more times than I can count.'

'Any disciplinary hearings though?'

'No, not one. That's what matters. I never get a 164. I never get punished...'

I inclined my head then took a piece of cheese

'Did Inspector Beedi tell you he wants to get me?'

'Uh-huh.'

'Did he ask you to compile a dossier?' Ruff whispered.

How did Ruff know about the dossier? My eyes widened, and I nearly choked on my cheese chunk.

'Don't worry, Skip. I know all about it. Sergeant Paddy Gallaher told me. He said the boss asked *you* to rake the dirt.'

What a disingenuous, two-faced, shit-head Paddy Gallaher proved to be. *Why did he feel the need to tell Ruff?* I was shocked by this revelation. I didn't know what to say. Thankfully, I was saved from further unwelcome thoughts by the return of Mrs. Eve Palmerston. She entered the lounge and announced: 'Supper is served.' Ruff gave a smile and allowed me to go into the back room first. We sat around a G-plan table and tucked into a sliced melon starter. Sweet and juicy.

'Lovely, Mrs. P' I told her. She smiled amiably.

After appetizers, she served gammon steaks with boiled potatoes and fresh peas. With more pineapple on the side. 'Very nice too,' I commented. For dessert, we had a generous portion of Arctic Roll. I folded my napkin neatly and announced, with genuine emotion, 'That was probably one of the best meals I've had in my life.' I meant it.

Eve shone with pride. She kissed her husband. We retired back to the lounge for a nightcap.

Ruff poured me a liberal portion of his best gold watch. I took the glass and had a sniff. 'Do you want water with that? Or are you straight?' Ruff's eyes sparkled.

'Straight is good.' I told him. 'I'm a straight man. You know that.'

Eve helped herself to a red Martini and a dash of lemonade. The three of us chatted for hours. We shared childhood reminiscences, and we talked about stupid things such as schooldays and holidays. We avoided discussing the Job. Once Ruff and I had finished the bottle of Scotch, I glanced at my watch and saw it had reached midnight. It was a discipline offence to be out of the section house after 12 p.m. I made an urgent noise to move.

'You want me to give you a ride to the sexual house?' Ruff mumbled.

'No, that's fine mate. I don't mind walking.'

'Nonsense. It will take a minute. I'll have a Jimmy Riddle and be right with you. You better not be late in.'

'Good of you.' I replied. I felt slightly squishy.

Once Ruff left the room, Eve Palmerston prowled over and gave me an unexpected kiss on the lips. She grinned cheekily into my face: 'Do not forget I have a long list of women who need dates. Let me know when I can fix you up.'

'Thanks, Mrs. P. It's been great to meet you. Thanks for a brilliant supper.'

'You're welcome, my love.'

Ruff returned with his car-keys. We stomped out, to jump into his cream-coloured Hillman Imp parked on the edge of the green. Mrs. P had already pulled her marigold gloves on, for the washing-up. I gave her a shy wave.

After a short trip to SQ28, Ruff crunched to the front doors of the Section House and ushered me out.

'There you are Skip. Door to door service.'

'Thanks for everything,' I told him.

'See you on night duty,' he replied. Then roared away.

I stumbled into the police hostel, feeling unsteady on my feet. Standing by the porter's hatch were two elegant females. Both wore tracksuit bottoms and fluffy tops. They examined me and provided toothy grins. 'Bints.' I said. 'This evening gets better and better.'

19

Hovis and the Fisherman's Daughter

The first thing I resolved to do, once I arrived for Night Duty, was to settle the contentious issue that seemed to be fermenting in my mind. I needed to confront Sergeant Paddy Gallaher about his double-dealing. He'd told Ruff about the dossier, and I felt irritated as hell about it: 'Why did you tell Constable Palmerston I have been asked to compile a report on him?' I demanded from the old Skipper when I saw him in the front office.

Paddy seemed unflustered by my assertive attitude and merely gave a nod of acceptance. 'Do not worry dear boy. Ruff would have found out eventually. You know how he operates — do you think his fore-knowledge will make one jot of difference? He has less self-control than a Bubble and Squeak at a plate-smashing party. If anything, I have strengthened your hand.'

'Strengthened? How so?'

'Well, now he's walking on ice, isn't he? He'll try extra hard not to slip-up — it's an odds-on bet he will *over*-compensate — that means he'll be tense. Ruff will be puckering so tight he's bound to make one giant fart of a mistake. And when he does, you'll be there to record the stink, eh? The additional pressure will cause him to make more blunders, not less.'

'However, I would have preferred it if you had kept *shtum*. Or at least you had warned me you were going to spill the beans to him.'

'Right, fair enough, son. Point taken. By the way — you haven't got too close, have you?'

'No.'

'Good. Cos' a little bird told me you went around to Ruff's gaff for dinner. And that's not right, is it? A Skipper can't be the mate of a P.C. That's the truth of it. Give them an inch and the constables will take a ruddy mile. You're best warned...'

Perhaps I'd judged Paddy too harshly. Maybe I'd come on too strong. After all, I was the probationary Sergeant, and Paddy was the longest-serving skipper on Q Division. I had much to learn. 'Sorry if I came over a bit anxious. A bit tense...' I explained. 'I didn't mean to sound so accusative.'

'Not a problem, son, I know how you feel. You have Beedi breathing down your neck. I'd feel the same in your shoes.'

After my chat with Sergeant Gallaher, I flicked through the stop book. I didn't find many stops, even less recorded in red, so I made the decision I would take it up with the relief team. Get them to buck their ideas up.

'By the way —' interrupted Paddy as I slapped the stop book shut, 'I'll be taking Fart'n Mart'n off the Panda for the next couple of shifts...'

'Oh?' Was Paddy Gallaher stirring the shit again?

'Yes,' continued Paddy 'I cleared it with the guv'nor.'

'Can I ask why you did such a thing? The guv'nor was clear to point out I was in charge of the section....'

'I need an assistant station officer on nights. Fart'n Mart'n is one hundred per cent suited to that role.'

'You need an assistant station officer?'

'The prisoners come in thick and fast on night-duty. I will be working extra-hard in the charge room, so I will need someone reliable to oversee the station office when I'm not there.'

'Of course.' I saw sense in that. 'But is Fart'n Mart'n the best man for the job?' I enquired.

Paddy confounded my expectations: 'Well, he's fucking useless on the streets —' the old Skipper shrugged, 'A fucking liability. I think he'd be more useful inside.'

I couldn't agree more.

Over tea, I told my relief they needed to do more stops and searches. 'I want to see more section sixty-six stops done. I want to see more entries in red. Okay?'

The Constable's nodded.

'Also — we are one Panda short this week because Fart'n Mart'n will be in the station office.' I heard a few grouses at my suggestion. I posted Dave Yale to the van and teamed him with Wally West. I had yet to work with Charlie Butler — known to his team-mates as 'M.C.' — so I assigned him to Panda Four and thought I might ride alongside. He rolled his eyes when I made *that* suggestion.

By 11:30 the relief had their first section sixty-six 'red-ink' arrest. Wally West called Quebec Mike to inform them he'd nabbed a man 'going equipped to steal.'

'That's the first red entry in our Stop Book,' he added.

'Good work,' I transmitted over the bat-phone.

Within minutes of Wally's arrest, Ruff called for the station van. It didn't surprise me. 'Van required for a male RC1. Detained for theft.'

'Yeah, I will come and get you,' offered Dave Yale.

'Thanks, friend,' replied Ruff.

Charlie M.C. Butler drove our Panda unhurriedly down Embassy Road. He randomly selected two RC3's in his headlights. 'Want to give them a tickle, Skip?' he asked

'I don't see why not. We can find out where they're going and what they've been up to...'

M.C. Butler pulled the Panda alongside the males. They didn't slow down — or even acknowledge his presence — so he needed to roll down his window and shout through it: 'Where are you lads going?' They didn't respond. They continued to stroll as if they hadn't heard him or seen the police car.

'Oi! I am talking to you two ignorant bastards. Where the fuck are you going?'

They disregarded him again.

'Silvery Moons. I hate them,' M.C. said, under his breath.

'Calm down, mate.' I said. 'It's the *way* you did it.'

'What does that mean?' The Constable stared at me with a look of sly hatred in his eyes. 'What the fuck do you know anyway? You're a numpty from C Division with temporary stripes on your arm.'

'Twat did you say? I cunt hear you,' I replied with my tongue in my cheek.

'What?' he responded.

'Stop the bloody car,' I barked.

Constable Butler continued to roll down Embassy Road.

'Didn't you hear me?' I shouted, 'I said, stop the bloody car.'

M.C. stamped his size ten boot on the brake pedal. This impulsive action almost shot me through the windscreen. Nevertheless, I managed to stay calm. 'Get out' I ordered. At first, the Constable didn't respond. He merely gave an angry look. 'Get out,' I repeated. I opened the door and alighted from the Panda. 'Shut the engine off,' I told him. I heard the engine go silent. Then I heard the click of the car-door opening.

I focused on the imminent arrival of the RC3s. The guys sauntered my way. 'Evening gentlemen,' I smiled. I held out my arms like a Landing Signal Officer might do onboard an aircraft carrier. I used my body to hinder their progress. I heard one of the RC3's suck his teeth. The other attempted to squeeze by. So, I grabbed his arm. He stared down at my hand as if it contained something foul. Then he gazed steadfastly into my eyes.

'Let go, Babylon. I do nuttin.'

'I want a chat. See where you're headed. What you're doing. Can you respect that?'

'We don't respect you. You only stop us because we is black.'

Not put off, I said: 'Where are you going?'

'Home.'

'From where?'

'A party in Craven Park Row...'

'You walk all the way?'

'What you fink hofficer? You fink me half-inch a car den walk?'

'That is bullshit,' the other said.

I became aware that a shadow-figure lurked close by my side. I hoped it was M.C.

'Well, have you?'

'Have we what?'

'Have you tea-leafed a car?'

I heard louder teeth sucking at this suggestion.

Then I heard the words I prayed for. 'You can search us if you don't believe us, bomboclaat dak.'

I glanced at MC. He returned a sheepish stare. I turned my attention to one of the RC3's. He'd already started to pull out his pockets to show they contained 'nuttin'.

'Constable Butler. Will you pat him down?' I suggested.

I went to the other suspect. I turned him around so I could feel along his shirt. He had a comb in his top pocket. I pulled out his wallet and told him to hold it. Then I felt along his waistband. I found a fiver in his back pocket, so I put the banknote into his palm for safekeeping. I patted his legs and even tucked my fingers into the tops of his shoes. He was clean.

'This one's clean,' said M.C.

'Great. Sorry lads. We're doing our job. We need to take a few details so you can be on your way.'

'Whatever man, just get on wiv it,' said the mouthiest of the duo.

After we had the information, we needed for a Stop Book entry, we left Embassy Road and took a call to a Bail Enquiry.

'See what one or toucan do...' I said. M.C. grinned. He had lightened-up, thank God! 'The lengths we go for pleasure, heh?' I added.

'Sorry, Sarge. I shouldn't have got my tits in a wringer.'

That was about as close as I would get to an apology from him, so I nodded. 'We'll leave it at that,' I suggested.

20

An emergency call was broadcast over our bat-phones as I completed a midnight cuppa with M.C. Butler back at the Nick.

Ruff took the call and asked Dave Yale to back him up. The report suggested that a car had crashed off the Wealdstone Bridge. It sounded interesting. I asked Charlie M.C. Butler to get me there.

By the time we arrived at the scene, Ruff, and Dave Yale had already blocked the road with their vehicles. I told M.C. to 'wave his arms around' a bit — by that time — the streets were empty anyhow.

Constable Dave Yale came over to tell me what he knew: 'It looks like the geezer driving the car over the hump-back bridge had a bit of bad luck —' he suggested.

'Really?'

'Yes. There's a small gap in the fence — his car sliced through it then slid down the slope. Then it went in the drink.'

'Drink?'

'Yes. Into the canal water.'

'I better take a look —'

'Oh... and one other thing Skip...'

'Yup.'

'The geezer is brown bread.'

'What do you mean brown bread?'

'You'll see.'

I nodded vaguely, but I didn't know what he meant. So, I wandered towards the unmistakable greenish yellow ray that was cast by a police-issue seek-and-search light. The powerful shaft was being beamed from one side of the road to the other. It lit bushes and masonry as it crisscrossed. The road was a single-track highway that rose to a slight hump. Near the peak of that hump, I distinguished, even in the dark, a border fence that had been knocked down. I went to the bit of the fence that was missing. Once I reached the hole, I investigated the blackness and saw a curious amber flicker beneath, down in the darkness. I scrambled down the bank, towards that amber flash, with caution. As I descended, I gradually made-out the outline of Ruff. The flashing orange light got more intense and compelling as I got closer to him.

On my journey down the gradient, I made-out where the car had tumbled. It had obviously crashed down the bank very recently — because I saw branches and twigs that had been freshly cracked and splintered in its wake. Near the dark water were tyre-marks in the damp turf. I arrived at a narrow strip of smoothness that separated the bank from the water. The track was like a towpath, only thinner. Ruff came towards me. He held the sizeable seek-and-search lamp. It was a heavy item, so he held it in both hands.

'Can you see the indicator lamp?' he asked.

'The blinking light? Yes.' Ruff was obviously referring to the hypnotic amber light.

'Keep watching it...' Ruff said. He pointed the lens of the heavy-duty searchlight towards the blinker. He tapped the main switch on the searchlight, and it illuminated the entire area with a bright white light. I could see the result of the accident. I could see how the damaged car had crashed off the road bridge and then plunged down the slope. I could also see that the vehicle was now submerged six feet below the surface of the inky water. Surprisingly, even though the car had sunken into those murky waters, the electrical system still had enough power to operate the car's indicator lamp. The bulb buzzed and fizzed beneath the ripples.

'He's a goner' Ruff said suddenly, making me jump.

I passed a hand across my face, 'The driver? My God, the driver is still in it?'

'He went down with it.'

'How do you know?'

'I went down to see ...'

'What?'

'I've been down there...'

I gazed at Ruff. I already knew he was a hero — but this was another thing altogether. A shocking admission. 'How?' I burbled. I gawked into his bloodshot eyes. He returned an odd, wide-eyed stare. So, I scanned him up-and-down and saw things I hadn't seen earlier: For example, he had no boots. He stood in bare feet. Then I saw that his uniform was sopping wet. After that, I appreciated he was shaking — giant shivers quaked across his body. As I studied Ruff, I heard him generate a series of bizarre cracking noises. I viewed his wet gingery hair again. *Then* I grasped what he'd bloody done: 'Shit, Christ, Ruff. We need to get you into the warm.' He looked at me, and his teeth started chattering.

'Dove, doesn't...' he babbled. 'Dove doesn't tell the guv'nor. I hew not to say —' Ruff's teeth rattled, and I thought he might collapse. He started talking gibberish. 'I try to give it a go...' he continued. 'I couldn't get him out of dare. I doven't have the strength. I mammy sorry. I couldn't frag the door open. He still dare. He still in dare in de dark. Dare in da drowned car. God, I sorry.'

'Don't worry Ruff. We'll get you dry and into the warm.'

'He's Hovis,' he concluded.

21

I called Dave Yale to bring a blanket to our position. I also called the duty officer. The Fatacc report had to be written.

Dave and I packed the curiously quiet Ruff into a blanket then discreetly sent him back to the nick in one of the warm panda's.

I stared the required paperwork at the scene then called the night-duty Black Rats out from Alperton traffic garage. They came quite quickly and began their accident reconstruction while Inspector Beedi called for Met photographers. 'Coroners like pretty pictures to look at…' he explained.

We waited until first light so the car could be lugged out of the canal safely, with the heavy machinery the Black Rats brought in. As the car was hauled up, pissing water from all the cracks, the Job smudger did his duty and clicked away. 'Who is going to get the body out of the dunked car?' Constable M.C. Butler asked me, as his face grew ashen grey and his eyes fixed on the inflated corpse in the driver's seat. He bared his teeth and added, 'Anyone but me.'

'It's a Skipper's job,' I said.

Once the vehicle has been winched onto the road, we let the rest of the water drain out. Then I completed the gruesome task of recovering the body. The driver was a white man aged about 30 years. We didn't have a C.V.I. report at that early stage, so we had no idea who the man might be. I went through his pockets but found no identification. Just small change and house-keys.

'We'll let the idle bastards on early turn sort it out. No doubt matey will be reported Misper during the morning. So, day-shift can do the sodding death message,' Inspector Beedi suggested. I arranged for an undertaker to remove the body and night duty C.I.D. from Quebec Delta to be informed.

These 'specialists' attended briefly. They chatted with the Black Rats for a while — then, after a quick nod in my direction — the morticians departed with the body and the C.I.D. whizzed off in their G.P. car. They didn't even bother going down the bank to see where the vehicle had slid into the drink.

I returned to Quebec Mike, where I found Ruff in his favourite place: The boiler room. He had his feet in a basin of warm water and his breath smelt of whisky.

'You OK mate?' I asked.

'That might have been me, Skipper,' he said.

'The man in the car?'

'Yes. A couple of sherbets too many. A distraction. Then a moment later, you are fish-food. Life is wild and heartless. Isn't it?'

'Ruff, you will live *forever*. Trust me.'

22

The Quack and the Elephant's Trunk

During the next nightshift, the young P.C. Peter Prince, our full-time area-car operator, brought in a breath-test arrest from Ascot Road. Without a doubt, the driver had been drinking. But, having said that, the arrested man seemed in control of his faculties. Nevertheless, Peter 'the Ponce' Prince had done the right thing. Constable Godfrey Lambert had stopped the suspect for a moving traffic offence, and he'd sent Peter prince 'to deal.' P.C. Prince had smelt liquor on the driver's breath, so the young officer had shoved a bag into the man's gob. The errant motorist provided a positive specimen of breath — he turned the crystals green. So, the man was detained and brought to Quebec Mike, to go through the detention process. No, we needed to get hold of a blood sample for analysis. A police doctor (the divisional surgeon) would need to be called.

'Could you help with this one?' Inspector Beedi said as he walked across the front office. 'Paddy Gallaher and Fart'n Mart'n are doing superfluous jobs for me...'

'No problem, sir,' I told him. I was tempted to ask what they were doing but thought it wise to keep *schtum*. I went into the Charge Room to see about the new prisoner.

———

I recorded the details of the driver onto one of our massive charge sheets. He gave his name as Ernie Kent. I found one of the drink-drive booklets in a drawer and leafed through it to make sure no joker had defaced the pages.

'You searched the prisoner yet, Peter?' I asked absently.

'When will I be free to go?' interrupted Mr. Kent.

'You will be released once you have completed the drink-drive process. Once you are found to be fit,' I told the motorist.

He nodded and peered at his shoes.

'I haven't searched him yet...' replied Peter Prince.

'Be a good lad then and empty his pockets. Put his shit on the counter. Then go and call for a divisional surgeon. Make sure you put a message on the station pad. Once you've done that come straight back.' Peter dumped the loose change, polo mints and keys he found in the man's skyrockets onto the side. Then he marched off to call for a doctor to take a blood sample.

'I opt for urine,' said the man, as I listed his property.

'I'll go through that in a moment. Once the doctor is here.'

'You do not need to call a doctor because I opt for urine.'

'Have you been through this process before Mr. Kent? I expect you have.'

'I might have. Who cares?'

'We'll find out anyway. You might as well tell me...'

'Five years ago.'

'Five years ago, what? Did you get disqualified?'

'Banned. Wasn't I? Two years.'

'How much have you had to drink tonight?'

'A bottle and a half.'

'Thanks for being honest. A bottle and a half of what? Brown ale? Lemon barley water? Tizer?'

'More like a couple of bottles, I suppose. Come to think of it.'
'Brown ale?'
'Something similar,' Mr. Kent replied.

23

Constable Prince came back with a 'carbon' copy of the message he'd sent. The message read: 'Divisional Surgeon required at QM to take a blood sample.' I smiled, impressed he'd taken the trouble to make himself 'a carbon.'

'Ruff told me to carbon everything...' he explained. 'Ruff taught me to keep my piece of carbon paper folded ready, in my pocket. Then I would be prepared. Like I was in the Cub Scouts.'

'That is good advice. We can pin the message to the paperwork.'

'Can I get my head down?' asked Mr. Kent.

'No, you can't...' I told him. 'You need to stay awake during the procedure.'

'Can I have a cigarette?'

'Not until we're done.'

'It does not seem right.'

'No, true, it doesn't.'

We waited for the Police Surgeon.

I got bored reading the latest edition of the 'Job' newspaper, but as I folded it away, we heard a massive crash from the station yard. The noise scared the holy bejesus out of us. It sounded as if the entire building had collapsed.

'What the fuck is that?' asked Mr. Kent with wide eyes. 'Are we under attack?'

'Do not alarm yourself, Mr. Kent. Constable Prince, see what caused that awful noise.'

'Yes, Sarge.'

'Peter. Be careful.'

I unlocked the back entrance to the Charge Room so the young P.C. could slip out into the dark and investigate the almighty din. Then I pulled the charge-room door to and gave the prisoner a warm smile, to reassure him.

24

Five minutes later, the door to the charge room swung open. In toppled a tall man wearing a grey suit. He dropped a large brown briefcase onto our polished linoleum floor, then staggered towards me. His breath smelled strongly of intoxicating liquor. 'Bollocks,' he said, by way of introduction.

Directly behind him stood Constable Prince who was giving me sheepish glance.

'Take the prisoner to the bench,' I told him.

'Sarge?'

The tall man remained on two legs, but his knees were decidedly shaky. It seemed apparent he couldn't stand upright much longer. He wavered like a poplar in a strong breeze.

'Take the prisoner to the bench. Before he falls ...' I ordered.

'Um?' said Constable Prince. He grabbed the tall man by the elbow and headed him towards the extended bench. Once he got him there, he pushed him down next to Mr. Kent, the alleged drunk driver.

'To whom am I fucking addressing myself?' asked the tall man, once he'd sat on the bench and extracted a chunk of wax from his left ear. He peered imprecisely in my general direction and seemed to experience difficulty recognizing me.

'Sergeant Chesterfield' I told him.

'Then you ought to know, sir, that the man now addressing your good fucking self — to wit: me, sir — is none other than the good Doctor Winston Reynolds of this parish and ilk.'

I was puzzled. 'Where is the arresting officer for this Elephant's Trunk?' I shouted.

'Sarge, there's something you should know...' whispered P.C. Prince

'Come here, Peter,' I said. 'I'd better not take my eyes off these two piss-heads, so you'll need to get close...' So, Constable Prince tiptoed to my side, scrutinized the whole while by the two drunken characters on the bench. They remained utterly motionless. They could hear a pin drop.

'The tall man is Doctor Reynolds,' Peter muttered.

Well, I knew that much already. He announced himself with elegance when he came in through the door — if not fully coherently.

'He's the Divisional Surgeon.'

'What the fuh?'

'He crashed his Jag into our wall.'

'Crashed?'

'Yes — when he drove into the police yard. He crashed into the wall of the nick. That's what made that awful din. I think his car's a write-off.'

'But he's fucking slaughtered,' I said, as I looked over at him. The doctor gave a shaky thumbs-up.

'Indeed, he is,' Peter Prince agreed.

'Where the fuck is or are the prisoners to which you want me to examine Sarjee's-Aunt?' asked the Police Surgeon. He slanted on the drunk's bench and looked at me with skewed eyes.

I glanced at the man sat next to him: A man who now seemed entirely sober in comparison. I turned my attention back to P.C. 'Constable Prince. Please escort the Police Surgeon to one of our cells. I recommend number three. After that, fetch Mr. Kent a nice cup of tea, will you? And offer him a cigarette.'

'Yes Sarge.'

'Two sugars, Mr. Kent?' I asked.

'That would be lovely,' said the first prisoner. He had a smile upon his face that wouldn't go away. I sighed as I tore up his charge sheet. After that I started to fill-in the person-at-station document for the *real* elephant's trunk — Doctor Reynolds.

25

Fly By Nights and the Dunlop Tyre

The next evening, I joined Ruff on Panda Three.

'I see the boss has allowed knob chops Fart'n Mart'n out on his own this evening,' Ruff commented, as we put-putted up the High Street in the little blue Morris Minor.

'Apparently, the Inspector wanted Fart'n Mart'n to go and take a statement from some fellow. A fisherman who might have witnessed the Wealdstone Brook fatacc...' I explained. 'I think the fisherman might be the original informant. He saw the car thunder into the water. He didn't bother to call the Old Bill 'til he got home. That's when he had a sudden attack of the moralities.'

'What a shitbox,' said Ruff.

I was going to say something along the lines of: *There's nothing you could have done to save him... you did your best.* But the words wouldn't come from my lips, for some reason. So, I shook my head and peered out of my window. We rumbled along the deserted backroads with the car lights off. Ruff used the handbrake so our rear lights wouldn't give us away.

'There has been a series of burglaries in this area...' he said. 'On drums that back onto the railway line... I would like to nick the son of a bitch responsible for 'em.'

'Indeed.' I was keen to change the subject, though also striving to remain vigilant. 'How's your old lady?'

'Me?' he gave me a swift glance, 'My Trouble? Why? She's moaning like a drain as usual. She complains she's got no bread and honey. Keeps on grousing: blah, blah, blah... we should return to the Black Country. To help her skin and blister run a laundry. She says we can both get good-paying jobs in the North of England. She says she could help her skin in the launderette while I could do odd-jobs around Wolves. She says we'd have a better life.'

'What do you think?' I asked.

'Me? I want to be a copper. I like this work. It's what I do.'

'Couldn't you join a force up there in the Black Country? Transfer to West Midlands?'

'Bit of a come-down, isn't it? Plus, they don't take kindly to transferees from the metro comical police farce up there. They think we're a bunch of scoundrels and cheats...' he looked my way again, 'Maybe they're right.'

'Don't they have wheeler-dealers in the Midlands?'

'They do — but they're sleepy and dull in comparison to you Cockney Sparrows down in the smoke. Anyway, if I went back home, I'd leave the Job. The pay is even worse in Northern forces. Plus, my trouble wants bin lids. And says she can't afford 'em on police pay. I don't doubt she'll eventually get her own way and I'll have to go back home start a new life.'

'Is that what you want?'

'Sometimes, *yes*. Yes, I do.'

'Like the other night?'

Ruff didn't answer. He just turned his nose up and made a grumbling sound.

So, we crawled the lanes and alleyways in silence, the pint-size Morris Minor crunching softly along empty paths until a call came out over the bat-phone. 'Any unit can deal with a lurker. Twenty-eight Park Drive. Female informant reporting a Peeping Tom. Anyone?'

'Yeah. We'll look. Show Panda Three assigned,' transmitted Ruff. Then he winked at me, 'OK Skip?'

'Yes, it could be fella responsible for the burglaries,' I suggested.

26

We arrived at number 28.

In fact, that's not true; actually Ruff pulled the Moggy short of the house we were supposed to attend. He switched off the engine before we approached, then coasted to a halt outside number 24. He began to get out of the police car: 'Do not slam the door, Skipper. *Click* it closed.' I nodded. 'Keys under the visor, as usual.'

Once clear of the vehicle, we moved in silence towards no. 28. At the dwelling, Ruff bumped the door with his shoulder to attract the attention of the occupier without making so much noise it would forewarn any lurker. A tasty looking bint came to the door. She wore a purple nightgown with a slit all-the-way-up one side. She looked smashing, and we both glimpsed her smooth pins through the smoky gauze. Her scotch eggs were elegant and shiny. 'Hello officers...' she said. 'The spectator is gone now. I heard a noise in the garden. I thought the racket might have come from a cat or a fox. I peeked out through a tiny slit in the curtains and saw the outline of a tall figure. He was hanging about near my washing line. I telephoned 999. They said he was probably a peeper.'

'No problem, love. We'll take a look around. We'll check the garden first,' said Ruff.

We crept around the building-line of her semi-detached house and warily pushed open a side gate. We went into the back-garden and padded onto grass that was wet with dew. We both looked up when we saw a chink of light from her upper window. The informant was obviously viewing us through a crack in her curtains.

'Look at this,' Ruff said.

I went to where he stood, by the clothes-prop. Ruff studied the turf. I twisted my head to see where he gazed, and I saw six clothes pegs abandoned on damp grass. We examined the clothing line. Two pairs of tights were hung-out to dry. After that, we returned to the front door of the house and Ruff banged his fist on the door. It opened quickly, and the bint who'd watched us from her window gave us a big smile.

'Do you have any washing on the line, love?' Ruff asked.

'As a matter of fact, yes, I do.'

'A couple of pairs of nylons? Anything else?'

'I do not remember exactly. Um? I think it was two pair of tights and three pairs of stockings.'

'Your stockings have been half-inched,' Ruff told her.

'Oh, God! That's not good. How do you know?'

'They're not on the line any more love. Detective work. Pegs on the grass... That's what the geezer was here for, we reckon. He's a knicker nicker. That's how we describe geezers like that *in the trade*.'

'I didn't have any knickers on...' said the bint, quite innocently.

'Well, quite' replied Ruff. He checked the length of her naked leg to authenticate the authenticity of her claim.

'We'll have to make a report,' I suggested, as I wrenched my eyes from the slit.

'Yup,' Ruff said, 'But not *yet* though Skipper, eh? We need to have a scout around the parish first. See if we might spot the tea-leaf.'

'While you do that, I'll get some cocoa going,' said the bint in the lingerie. 'By the time you get back, you'll need a hot drinkie...'

———

We hurried to the Panda parked up the road, and Ruff explained his plan. 'We know he didn't piss-off in *that* direction because that's where we came from. So, the geezer must have had it on his toes the other way —' Ruff indicated The Curve. 'He most likely panicked when he saw her looking out the window.'

'You don't think he's a burglar then?'

'No. This is the work of an amateur. A pervert. A dirty old man. Like I told her: A knicker nicker...'

We drove bit by bit up 'The Curve' and into Myrtle Grove. There was no sign of anybody around. All quiet. We drove down the streets and avenues that connected Park Drive with High Road. They were all clear too.

'Better go back to the crumpet' Ruff said. 'Let's have a drink with her and take details of the beat crime.' I agreed with a nod, so we turned into the busier High Road and Ruff positioned the car to perform a 'U' turn when something caught his eye. 'Hello, hello, hello,' he muttered.

I twisted my neck to figure out what he'd noticed. I saw an elegant lady dressed in a neat, black-twin set. I guessed she was walking briskly back to her apartment. She held a reedy cigarette in one hand and a shiny little shoulder bag in the other.

Ruff abandoned the turnaround manoeuvre and headed instead for the stylish woman. He drove a little way past her. Then came to a halt. He jumped out of the Panda, to cut her off: 'Good evening, ma'am. Can we have a word?'

The lady paused. She smiled kindly —her teeth gleamed in the street-light. She appeared tall and fine-looking, well maintained, and she possessed an air of easy elegance. She even gave me a coquettish smile. But didn't answer Ruff's question.

'Where have you just come from?' Ruff asked.

She indicated behind her. She used a perfectly manicured, slender finger to point *that away* but never said anything. Instead, she took a puff from her slim-line cigarette.

'What you got in your handbag, honey?' Ruff said.

The lady seemed irritated by the question. She shrugged. But didn't provide an answer.

'Don't say much, do you love? Has a kitty-cat got your tongue?'

She shrugged again.

'May I?' Ruff said. He took hold of the handbag and forced it open.

'What have we here, poppet?' Ruff pulled out a pair of silky, clean-smelling stockings.

'Mine' uttered the lady.

'What?'

'They're mine?'

'Whose?'

'Mine,' she said again.

'Got a deep voice for a woman, haven't you?' Ruff remarked. He pulled out two more pairs of expensive-looking nylons. At that stage, the 'lady' started to cry. Her mascara started to run.

'Give her a search, a quick once over...' Ruff told me. 'I will tidy up the back of the car for her.'

I took the handbag from the lady and patted her down. She had nothing in her pockets. Once the silky stocking was taken out of her bag, it only contained mints, a key to a door, two florins and a bus ticket.

Ruff led the 'lady' to the Morris and shoved her in the back seat.

Once we were all comfy in the minuscule car, he explained the situation: 'At this moment, my love, you are nicked for theft of stockings. You're not obliged to say anything. Et cetera. Et cetera. You know the words...' She sobbed when she heard this. He went on: 'However, pay attention carefully. We may be able to come to a suitable agreement. But it requires you to fully cooperate with us. Do you want to go down the nick?'

The lady shook her head with vigour.

'From now on, sweet pea — you must speak when you are spoken to — understand? If you do not speak to me, you will go down the road to our factory. Yes?'

'Yes,' came a hoarse voice.

'What's your name?' asked Ruff.

'Benny Lestari' said the voice of a man.

'Are you married, Ben?'

'Yup.'

'How long?'

'Seven years'
'Does your wife know about all this night-time tom-foolery?'
'No, officer.'
'Give the Sergeant here your full name and address and your date of birth.'

I took note of Benny's details.

'Never been in trouble with the police before, have you, Ben?'
'No, sir' he replied.
'If you told me porky pies you will be found out. Are you certain you've never been in trouble before?'
'Never.'
'Well, here is the situation, Ben: You are banned from this neighbourhood. We are going to run you out of town. If we ever see your scrawny arse in the area again, we will lift you. Got that? And you'll be charged with tonight's crime. Understand?'
'Yes.'
'If we get more reports of stuff nicked from washing lines, we will be around your house pronto. We will tell your wife about your nocturnal adventures. And we will disclose this to your employer. So there better be no more bleeding thefts in this area or you'll be coming to see where we work. *Capeesh* darling?'
'Crystal, officer.'
'Good. Well, on this occasion, you can scoot off on your twinkling daisy-roots. But you'd better count yourself incredibly lucky. We do not want to see you again ...'

Ruff jumped out, then pulled the tranny from our Panda and pushed her back on the street, faced in the direction of home. He slapped her backside and said, 'Go on honey, off with you...'

Ruff jumped back into the Moggy. 'Right, Skipper, we have a hot-date with a semi-dressed bint and a cup of cocoa ...'

'Uh-huh.'

'I wonder how she'll thank us when we return her nylons.'

'She'll be extra grateful...' I suggested.

27

The most exciting call you can get on night-duty shift is the thrilling 'Suspects on.' It means a burglary is *actually* in progress. The request is often made by the occupant of a raided house, most generally from a room upstairs — but sometimes from a neighbour who has seen a criminal climb through a window. Whatever the circumstances, it is one of the emergency calls that *everyone* attends. All the coppers on duty will get to the location of a *Suspects On* in super-quick time...

Before long that exact call came in: 'All units, all units from Quebec Mike. Two-two, twenty-two Gallahers Avenue. Suspect on premises. Time of origin zero three five eight. All units respond. Quebec zero and other R/T units have already accepted.'

In most cases even police units from other stations would make rapid progress to the scene. In all probability the van, wireless car and dog-van would have already responded via the main-set radio and would be using their blue lights and gong to get through traffic. (The wireless car rarely utilized their fitted two-tones during the night. The *twos* were very disruptive and the noise tended to alert suspects to their approach.) Usually, the Comms officer would warn officers: 'Turn off blues. No blues and twos for this one, please. Silent approach. Repeat, silent approach.'

Panda-cars would use what limited emergency equipment they

had available — in other words, they'd turn on their illuminated 'police' signs on the roof. And make generous use of beep-beep horn and headlights.

We arrived *after* the wireless car and van but *before* any of the others. Which was to be expected. Because to arrive first at a 'Suspects On' call was a matter of pride and often the lifeblood of canteen-discourse for days: 'Did you see that Misty got to the scene last?' somebody might say, with a laugh. 'I arrived after the wireless car but before the dog van...' someone else might claim. 'I was the first Panda on the scene, though,' another officer might brag. 'I got to the place in under two minutes...'

So, we rolled into the street, the engine already cut-off. The Morris came to a gliding handbrake stop some thirty yards short of number 22. Ruff hid the keys under the visor. He motioned that I should follow.

'We'll go up the side of the house...' he whispered. 'See if we can get into the back garden. Slide up the bank at the rear...' I grunted. 'Turn you bat-phone down low —' he added. 'Radio crackle travels hundreds of yards. If he hears it, the burglar will be of like a shot...'

I gawked at my talking brooch fixed to my epaulette. An officer could select three different volumes using a small grey toggle — Position 1: annoyingly loud. Position 2: dangerously quiet.

Position 3: total silence.

I selected option 3.

We scurried to the side of the rear garden to number sixteen — it might have been number fourteen, I can't remember — but it was Gallaher's Avenue. We avoided a kiddie's swing, a sandpit and a Wendy house. We arrived at the far end of the garden where we found a patch of gooseberries and other assorted soft-fruit trees. We crashed our way through the bushes and found ourselves standing at a dilapidated — but high — fence. It stood pale and stark and impeded our progress. It reckon it must have been six-foot tall. I thought we'd have to turn around and try another garden. But suddenly the fence-panel collapsed under the persuasive weight of Ruff's right shoulder. 'Look at that...' he said drolly. 'What the fuck? It fell. Must have been the wind, I suppose. The occupants will come and fix it in the morning.'

We stepped through the gap he'd made and onto the bank. We scrambled through mouldy cabbages and festering compost till we arrived onto the train lines.

'Be careful, Skipper,' Ruff told me. 'The trains are still coming — the line isn't turned off yet. Keep sharp and stay on the clinker. And, whatever you do — *never* cross the tracks.' I think I gave him a wide-eyed stare and took a gulp.

We gazed down the railway line towards where we imagined the rear of number 22 might be. That's where the suspect was last seen.

'Better wait here,' whispered Ruff. 'See what develops.'

The hoped-for developments materialized almost instantaneously. First, we heard a dog bark. An unusual woof. Acute and practically a puppy-like squeal.

'Fantastic —' Ruff said. 'That's Spirit. The bitch can raise a pickaxe handle in her mouth. She's a formidable bow-wow. My favourite police dog on the Force. I recognized that doggie-bark right away…' I appeared confused, so Ruff added: 'Her name is Spirit. She's got the scent of the suspect. That's her noise… her way of showing that she's onto something.' I felt the excitement bubble inside my guts.

Thirty seconds later, we heard a louder, barking noise. This time a proper woof. 'That's Spirit again. She's indicating.'

'Indicating?'

'Yes, telling her handler — Dave Sharrow — that she found the fucker. She sniffed him out. Good girl…'

Then we heard shouts. Lots of shouts. We couldn't make out what was being hollered, but suddenly the night-air was full of yells, and the noise started to wake up dozing householders. Lights flickered on, other dogs barked, and roosting birds became agitated. Even the wind seemed to pick up.

Then we saw a shape. It emerged ahead of us on the railway line.

The impression was just a shadow at first. A shadow that had — without explanation — come to life. I rubbed my red-raw eye-sockets to get a better look. I remember being irritated by the wind because it blew directly into my face. I gazed at the apparition. And became sure it was a man standing on the tracks. He started to come our way. I also became aware that Ruff pulled his stick from his trouser pocket. As he extended the truncheon from his secret pocket, where the length of wood remained concealed, he said: 'He's on his way, Skipper. Better get ready. Get your stick out... He'll want to fight.' I tugged at the leather strap on my truncheon and, simultaneously, I broke wind.

'Hmm! Hmm! Baked later to taste fresher,' commented Ruff.

A few seconds passed then the shadow-man hesitated. He faltered.

'Bollocks. He saw us,' whispered Ruff. 'Or maybe he smelt your fart. You dirty bastard...'

As Ruff uttered those words, the man started running. Diagonally across the dangerous railway-track. He headed for the other side. Away from the coppers and dog barks. Good tactics, I thought.

I turned my head to glance at Ruff, to see what we should do next, and I couldn't believe what I saw... he run across the rails. In hot pursuit.

'Christ almighty,' I said aloud. 'I thought we were *not* supposed to cross the tracks.' I tried to keep a beady eye on Ruff. But I also wanted to see where the suspect might be headed. I looked at the rails and remembered thinking I didn't want to step on a live-rail or get my foot caught in a trap. I didn't fancy getting knocked down by the early morning express to Birmingham.

The suspect disappeared, he crashed down a slope, hastily followed by Ruff. I admit I was more cautious than the Constable. But decided I would have to go. So, I tip-toed across the tracks, straggling a few yards behind.

Once I arrived on the other side, I heard the crash and crunch of twigs. And I saw both figures bounce from the rail-bank and into more back gardens.

I thought I caught a glimpse of Ruff bounding along behind the suspect so followed as nimbly as I could. I grabbed my tunic on some hidden barbed-wire, and it shredded my sleeve to bollocks.

The hunt was still on. I heard a crash and smash as Ruff fell-through a garden fence and knocked over a garden ornament.

For a while thing went quiet. I made-out some distant barks and a few bird chirps. Then I recognized the snap-and-crackle of a police radio ahead. Just like Ruff had said, the radio sizzle was easily heard above other noises. I headed for that tell-tale noise.

I ran through a garden, jumped a side-gate that refused to budge and twisted my ankle on the way down before I scuffed my boots to buggery. My hands were red-raw. I must have grazed them on a concrete post. I found myself standing in another suburban street, one that I didn't recognize. Ruff stood in the roadway just ahead of me.

'Shhh!' He said. He was irritated by the noise I created. I listened for the suspect.

'I'm sorry,' I said, as I trod towards him.

'I chased that son of a street whore into this road…' he whispered. 'But he's gone to ground. I have called Dave Sharrow and Spirit. They are on their way. Where is that wankerdickknob Fart'n Mart'n when you need him? We need *all* our units here! We need to search and secure both sides of the railway. The burglar might even double-back. We need to get everyone down here on the hurry up.'

28

Ruff called up on his personal radio: 'Quebec Mike one from four-one-three. Do you know the current location of one-twenty Fart'n Mart'n? I can't raise him on the bat phone.'

'He was asked to do a job earlier. That was before midnight. I haven't seen him since,' replied the Inspector.

'Confirm — is he at the station? Or on the ground? Because we haven't seen him tonight, over...'

'Four-one-three, he's not at the station tonight. Like I said already, he is dealing with an enquiry for me — he's on the ground.'

'Out to you. Quebec Mike — what's the last job you assigned one-twenty please?'

'Four-one-three. Just to let you know that Fart'n Mart'n has not accepted any calls tonight. We were told, by the Duty Officer, to keep him free. It's been authorized by Inspector Beedi.'

'Received. I can't raise Fart'n Mart'n on the radio. Do you think you might try for me? We need *all* available units down here for this burglary suspect. He's gone to ground. We had a foot chase, and now he is hiding. We need to complete a street search.'

'Received.'

'Four-one-three. Do you want *me* to make my way down? Can I be of any assistance?' asked the boss, Inspector Beedi. Now Ruff found himself between a rock and a hard place. He couldn't exactly turn down the kind offer from the Inspector. Especially since he'd made such a song-and-dance about the absence of Fart'n Mart'n. On the other hand, the guv'nor was the very last person we needed down here, fucking things up. As expected, there was a pause before Ruff replied. 'Yes, sir. That's affirmative. Please keep in contact with the area car or dog van. They'll tell you where you need to be.'

'Got it four-one-three. Understood. Out.'

———

I became aware that none of those radio transmissions had come out of my 'talking brooch.' I'd heard them all on Ruff's P.R. though. I peered down at my brooch and decided that, maybe, my radio had turned itself so low I couldn't hear it. Ruff checked me over.

'Fuck, you're a state Sarge...' he said, as he shook his head in dismay. 'You are bleeding too. Your jacket is torn. And it seems you lost your radio.'

'What?' I could see the talking brooch on my lapel. What was Ruff on about? *No, I hadn't lost my radio... had I?*

'The battery-pack is gone mate...' he said. 'It must have got ripped off when you were running. Probably it's somewhere on the rail tracks.'

'Shitfuck,' I said. If I lost my radio, it would mean a discipline enquiry. It would mean fine of two days' pay. I could even lose my stripes over something like this. 'I've got to retrace my steps, see if I can find it,' I told Ruff. 'Or the guv'nor will have my guts for garters.'

'You do what you got to do. I'll wait here for the dog-van and the wireless car.'

'Are you sure?'

'Yes. Go ahead.'

———

I did my best to retrace my steps because I needed to find my police radio. It had become detached from the microphone wiring during the last few minutes. This time I proceeded much slower across the gardens and back towards the rail-rack. I examined the ground along the way and decided my lost radio must be somewhere near the many hurdles I had vaulted across. Doubtless, it lay near where the barbed wire had ripped my jacket.

I made my way back to where the chase was in full swing. I took my time and paid full attention to the task. I carried out a meticulous search, but it proved fruitless. When I arrived at the railway tracks, I stopped, looked and listened. Like they advise you to do when you arrive at an unmanned level crossing. I should have done that earlier, I suppose, and I scolded myself. That's the danger of red-mist — you lose your common sense.

I couldn't hear anything coming, so I did my best to follow the diagonal path I had previously taken across the rail-tracks. I kept one eye on the ground and the other out — looking for trains. When I got to the opposite side, I found myself near the garden of number 16 Gallaher's Avenue. I experienced the roar of an express train as it *whooshed* past. The speed and power of the train scared the holy *bejabbers* out of me. The effect of the wind-rush and the resulting suction nearly dragged me from my feet. Only moments before, I had stumbled across those same rails. I would have been cut-to-pieces if it had arrived just seconds earlier. 'Bloody hell,' I declared.

I clambered down the cabbage slope and found the broken-down fence that Ruff had 'helped' to collapse earlier. And, of course, *that's* where I found my missing radio. It had detached itself right at the very start of events. *What a shitter.* Sod's law…

It seemed the talking brooch end of the gubbins, that's the part with a microphone on it, had somehow disconnected itself from the main battery pack. I managed to locate the connector in the gloom. So, I clicked it in and screwed it down. I pressed the squelch button. *Hey, presto!* I heard the familiar *schrrr* sound. *My bat-phone was working again.* I felt adequately relieved. So, I called up Ruff: 'Four-one-three from Seven-six receiving?'

'Go ahead' he muttered, pissed-off, once again because I disturbed his silence.

'Item recovered. I will return to the Morris Panda car. See you when you get back.'

'Understood. Wait there till I return,' he said brusquely.

29

It would be foolhardy — complete idiocy — to try to cross the tracks again. So that's why I chose to return to the Morris.

I wandered to our little Panda and, when I arrived, felt glad that Ruff habitually left the doors unlocked. I now saw sense in his idea of leaving the keys under the sun-flap. I eased myself into the passenger seat and examined my face in the rear-view mirror. My forehead had been gashed by barbed wire. But the blood felt dry. I studied my hands. *Grazed and scraped to bollocks.* I ached all over. I pushed back into the little seat of the Moggy and closed my eyes. I felt absolutely cattle trucked.

It must have been thirty minutes, maybe longer — when I heard a vehicle approach.

I opened my eyes, rotated my shoulders, and unfolded my arms. The motor halted right behind. I saw the dog-van, Quebec Zero. I glanced in the wing-mirror of our Morris to see Ruff get out of the van's passenger side. The driver's door opened and the dog-handler — Constable Dave Sharrow — stepped out int the early morning air.

I creaked open our Panda door and left the warmth of my seat to topple-over and greet them.

'Everything OK Sarge? You look a ruddy mess...' said Ruff. 'Your eyes are as red as a baboon's arse.'

'Yeah. I found my radio. Here in *this* back garden.'

'That's lucky. I didn't expect you'd ever get that fucker back.'

I became aware that the dog-handler, Dave Sharrow, had opened the doors of his dog van.

'What's the update?' I asked.

'We sent the dog for a sniff around. Spirit got confused. She started to follow *our* scent — yours and mine —over the rail line. Obviously, we couldn't risk her going on the rails.' I gazed at him in amazement. *It had been safe enough for us to cross* I pondered *but too dangerous for a dog.*

'We abandoned the tracking because of the hazards. Beedi is on the other side of the tracks,' Ruff explained, 'I asked Dave the handler to bring me back to you.'

'Thanks,' I said. 'How long do we wait? How long do suspects tend to go to ground?'

'I have known burglars to hide in a shed or coal bunker for hours. Literally. We must wait here until six o'clock. Beyond six, the early turn lads will start to turn up; they'll want their vehicles back.'

As Ruff said these words, I heard police dog 'Spirit' woof strongly.

'Shush now girl,' said her handler, 'You'll wake the whole darn parish.' But the police dog had not done. She started to spring about in her cage and bark wildly.

'That's strange,' commented the handler. He had a curious expression on his face. He opened the cage and let his dog out. Spirit bounded from the van and rushed straight towards our Panda car.

Everything was over in seconds.

We heard a scream. Followed by a high pitch whine. Then a long, hard yelp. Finally, we listened to the words: 'Get it off. Get the bugger off. me'

Police dog 'Spirit' had located 'Burglar Bill.' Guess where? He had been hiding beneath our Panda car all the while. The same Panda I had dozed in for about half-an-hour.

'What the fucking fuck?' I said.

Constable Sharrow dragged the prisoner from under the wheels. The dog went crazy; she yapped and sniffed. Her long tongue dripped with the goo that also drawled all over the prisoner's face.

'How come you didn't hear him? Under the car?' Ruff asked.

'I, er...' I shrugged. 'I don't know mate. He must've somehow got here before I arrived and kept quiet. I must have surprised him when I got inside the car noiselessly. He must have been waiting in silence all that time, hoping I'd go...'

'That must be it,' grinned Ruff. 'Quebec Mike, Quebec Mike. One arrest for burglary. I repeat — one in custody. Four-one-three out.'

We heard clapping over the airwaves, followed by remarks such as: 'well done' and 'Ace.'

Even Quebec Mike One, the Inspector, joined in with the show of appreciation. He sounded pleased as Punch: 'Thanks, Ruff. All units stand down. An arrest has been made. Can we get the van to Ruff's location? Ruff explain where you are now so we can get a van to you.'

While we waited for the van, Dave Sharrow and Ruff argued about who would 'take' the body to the Nick. The arrest was actually the dog's prize, truth-be-told. But the decision was made: Ruff would show himself as arresting officer and include Dave on the Charge Sheet as 'assisting officer.' That meant the body would 'count' on Dave Sharrow's work record, but he didn't have to do any of the shitty paperwork. Additionally, the handler needn't hang around the nick all morning. Whereas it would now be a long hard day for Ruff because he'd have to process the prisoner and possibly even take him to court.

'Do you want me to stay and help?' I offered.

'You need to go get your face stitched up, Sarge. Get yourself down to accident and emergency. Get them to look at that ugly boat-race. Looks nasty...' Ruff grinned.

'Really?'

'At least get a needle up your rusty trombone,' he added, 'For the fucking tetanus.'

'Shit.'

The van arrived, and the prisoner got slung into the back. When searched, he was clean — so if he'd nicked anything, he must have hidden it someplace.

Ruff located the Panda keys, still under the visor, and it was then that I reflected that perhaps it was a good job I'd gone back to the car after all. What if the burglar had found our keys? Can you imagine? We started to travel back to the nick: 'He could have fled in our car if I hadn't come back...' I offered.

'Yes. Tonight, the score is one-nil to Old Bill.'

Ruff seemed abundantly pleased with himself. And was still broadly smiling when he, unexpectedly, and very brusquely shouted: 'Fucker.' He rammed his foot so hard onto the brake pedal that I almost shot through the windscreen.

'What is it, Ruff?' I yelled.

Ruff turned the Panda around and made the tyres screech. He roared along the road we'd just driven down and ignored my question. I saw a murderous glint in his eyes. He did a hard left and rushed down a crumbled path that led to a line of detached garages. In the pale morning light, I saw the unmistakable turquoise rear-arse of a Met Police Austin Panda. The car was stuffed in tight, by a set of metal dustbins. It had been well hidden from view so Ruff must have used extraordinary vision to have even glimpsed it.

We jumped out of our Moggy and went straight to the steamed-up windows of the police car. 'Who is it?' I asked. 'Who's in there asleep?'

'My mate Marmite,' replied Ruff.

Inside the panda, I saw the scrunched and rumpled body of Fart'n Mart'n. Ruff tugged open the driver's door, and Fart'n almost fell out.

'Wakey, wakey sunshine,' Ruff shouted.

Fart'n shook his head and yawned. 'Hello, Ruff. What's up?'

'It's time to go off duty Farting. You've missed all the fun.'

'Have I?' Fart'n said, half yawning. 'What's happening?'

'Suspects on. Burglary. Foot chase. One arrested. What have you been doing you all this time? You bone-idle wank-splash. We've been calling you over-and-over. Haven't we Sargie? We needed you earlier. What have you been doing?'

'Gathering my thoughts before returning to Quebec Mike.'

'Gathering your thoughts? What fucking thoughts have you got in your dimwit mind that require gathering? You idle fuck...'

'My special assignment, cleared by the Inspector.' Fart'n Mart'n explained while he looked to me for sympathy and support.

'You're a fucking Dunlop Tyre.' I said. I turned my back on him.

Me and Ruff headed back to our Moggy. We rumbled down the alley, to return to the nick *pronto*.

'That was sweet as the moment the pod went pop...' commented Ruff, with a smile.

30

The Rub-A-Dub and the Betty Grables

'What time did you get off?' I asked Ruff as I sipped my sweet tea. On the previous night-shift, Ruff had nicked the burglar who'd evaded police by hiding under the very-same Panda car I had dozed in. I admit I still felt somewhat ashamed.

'About three o'clock...' he replied. 'The trouble wasn't pleased. Bless 'er. She refused to make my din-dins. The geezer got himself remanded in cus. The creeping insects took over the job. They found a string of burglaries to pin on him. They think he'll cough. He'll want them taken into consideration. He has a lot of form. Proper little fucking villain.'

'Nice job,' I said. The other chaps agreed. And made thumbs-up signs

'Skipper, since I've been such a good lad — top of the class, and all that — do you mind if I ask you a favour?'

'What is it?'

'Do you mind if I have a go on the van tonight. It's that I promised to do a little job for Charlie 'M.C.' Butler. I need to use the van to get the job done.'

'I suppose so since you asked nicely,' I said. 'But I want you to share van duties with Dave Yarrow from now. Don't hog it. Take it in turns.'

'Yeah! I get that,' said Ruff. 'Can I take M.C. with me? I need someone with strong-arms.'

'No,' I said, in a resolute tone. Because I didn't want him to have things all his own way. 'I require M.C. Butler to drive a Panda. You can take *me*.'

The surrounding Constable's eyeballed me when I said those words. Had I out-smarted and perhaps even out-played the man-of-the-hour?

'You're a clever rascal, Skipper,' Ruff commented.

31

We left Quebec Mike in the station van and made our way to a public house called The Anchor. It's situated on the main roundabout.

'This is the place...' Ruff grunted. 'There they are...' He drove the past the pub garden.

'What?' I asked. I couldn't see what the hell he was referring to.

'We'll collect them later. When it is a bit more relaxed.'

I expressed indifference as best I could. But I think I might have tutted.

'Fart'n Mart'n is back inside tonight. Performing non-essential jobs.' Ruff told me. 'Five officers in the nick. I would place ten sovereigns, odds-on, they're having a right good Tommy Tank in there. Makes a mockery of police unavailability doesn't it, Skipper?' He sighed. 'Half the fucking team are indoors. It makes me cry.'

'Well, don't assume I won't post *you* inside one day.'

'Fine by me,' Ruff said. 'Quality Street was made for sharing, after all.'

'I was thinking of posting you to gaoler next late turn duty anyway. How do you fancy that?' I tested the water.

'I'll do whatever you want, Skipper. You know that.' Ruff sideglanced me with a shrewd expression. 'Whatever you think is best.'

32

Around two in the morning, we returned to the Anchor public house. Ruff drove the van onto the grass, then parked between road and building. Perhaps to obstruct any view of what was about to happen. Ruff jumped out and listened for traffic. 'Bit busy here,' he stated. 'What with the roundabout and what-have-you.' He tramped around the garden-cum-car park to examine the wooden tables. They seemed haphazardly scattered around. He reviewed the hodgepodge of mismatched furniture. To me, they appeared stained with birdlime and drilled by a million cigarette burns.

Ruff went back to the van and pulled open the double-doors. I watched as he did this. 'Good of you, Skipper,' he shouted, 'To help in this way.' He glanced my way, 'Good of you to volunteer your services, I mean. A lot of supervisory officers would have said 'No' — but you're a bit special.' He smiled. 'Anyway, help me to get these fucking pub tables loaded into the van.'

'What?' I looked at the dilapidated tables.

'Come on, Skipper. Grab one. Put your muscle into it. We need to get them shifted *pronto*.'

'Into the van?' I asked.

'Where else?'

'But these belong to the pub!'

'They used to...'

I dropped an end of the first table and gazed at Ruff. 'What do you mean they *used* to?'

'The landlord is getting new garden furniture. He said we could help ourselves to these ancient fuckers. Charlie M.C. Butler promised his old Mum a new picnic set for her garden. So, I said I would arrange a special delivery for her. Make a nice surprise for the old dear. Won't it?'

'The landlord knows about this, right? This, er, appropriation?'

'Of corpse he does! You didn't suppose we'd were tea-leaving 'em did you?'

'Well, the thought crossed my mind,' I admitted.

'No. It's kosher. Folk around here like to help Old Bill.'

'I'd noticed.'

'So, help me shift the fuckers into the ruddy van, would you? We haven't got all poxy night.'

We removed two tables and eight of the best chairs. Ruff slammed the back doors shut once we'd completed the task. 'Why have we be doing this at two a.m.?' I asked. 'It still seems a bit dodgy if you ask me... '

'Well, the Betty Grables would have been used by Billy Bunters earlier, wouldn't they?' Ruff reasoned. 'And anyway, it's quieter now. Not much chance of us being called on to take-in a prisoner.'

'Fat chance of that...' I said to myself.

'What?'

'I had noticed it's only you and Dave who do any thief-taking on this relief. The others avoid detaining or even stopping criminals.'

'The others are okay. We can't all be thief-takers. Horses for courses, as they say.'

'Now you sound like Inspector Beedi,' I replied.

'God, I hope not.'

―――

We roared off while the tables rumbled in the back. We sped towards Harlesden. 'We are a long way from our beat,' I told Ruff. I grew concerned that we had travelled so far from QM division.

'Yes, as I said: It's kind of you to help in this way. You're a nice guy,' he winked.

We arrived in a suburban street and found number twelve. 'This is Mrs. Butler's place.' We halted outside, then dragged four chairs and a table into her front garden. Where we abandoned them.

'And the others?' I asked.

'On yeah. They're for Dave Yale's gaff,' Ruff replied. 'we'd better get them up there. Now.'

'Where?'

'Rickmansworth.' Ruff said. That was ten miles in the opposite direction.

I realized, then, with all certainty, that Ruff retained the upper hand.

the Betty Grables

33

'Well, is he dodgy or what?' Inspector Cliff Beedi snarled. He had called me in for *a chat*, during the last shift of night duty, and had asked me to join him in the teleprinter room. He expected the J-bells test to come in and *had* to be present for *that* message. 'I asked you to watch over Ruff and compile a dossier. So, what did you come up with?'

'Well, I admit his methods are a bit unorthodox,' I said, combing my hair with my fingers. 'I guess Ruff could be best described as unconventional. But he's an effective Copper.'

'Yes. But have you collected the dirt on him?'

'Well, yes and no. I started to compile a dossier as you asked and I have been shadowing him, as per your request. Like you suggested, I recorded everything I've seen.'

'Anything juicy? Have you uncovered anything that will send him down for a long stretch?'

'Send him down?'

'Yes. Indicted. Got anything delicious on him?'

Strewth, the Inspector must really hate him. He *actually* wanted to put him behind bars. 'Sir, might I remind you that Ruff is a married man. Are we really trying to do his legs to that extent?'

'I will settle for him to be thrown out of the Job...' said Inspector Beedi with a sigh. 'But I need something good and solid.'

'Very good, sir.'

'A little bird tells me that Constable Palmerston got a little soggy at the Fatacc at Wealdstone Brook. Can you confirm or deny that?'

'I know nothing sir,' I said, as I inspected the polish on my boots.

'Why is that?'

'I was not with him at the time. I arrived at the scene later.'

'I thought you said you were shadowing? I told you to keep a close beady eye on him, didn't I?'

'You did, Sir.'

'What he did *that night* was completely out-of-order. A comprehensive *no-no*. He should *never* have taken to the water. Think about what might have happened! Can you imagine the cover of the currant-bun, the next day, if things went wrong? 'Hero Cop drowns in River' would have been their headline. You and me, we'd be hauled up to the Commissioner's Office. And the Comish would have torn out our souls. There'd be no blue medal ribbons for us. Oh no, we'd be on lollipop patrol for the rest of our days. What remained of those days anyway... because the two of us would voluntarily jump from our kitchen stools, electric cables tied around our necks, just to leave it all behind — the constant, gnawing shame and the fucking ignominy....'

'Yes, sir, I think you've made your point.'

'Have I? The point is — don't let him out of your sight. Ever again. Got me?'

'Yup.'

'Anyway, that was a good arrest for burglary the other night, I will give him that. Ruff is an excellent thief-taker.'

I was pleased to hear this news, so I smiled. His comments made me feel a tiny bit better. But Inspector Beedi hadn't finished: 'Mind you, a little bird told me the villain had been found under the Panda car you were sitting in. Is that true?'

Who were all these fucking little birds? 'Yes sir, it's true. The police dog tracked the thief to my location.'

'Really? What were you doing in the Panda?'

'Resting.'

'Resting? Fuck me.' Beedi gave me a very unnerving stare: 'Let's get this straight. You were in the Panda having a doze while the rest of us were running around like blue-arsed flies trying to find the shit who was under your fucking nose all along? Is that the extent of it?'

'I, um ...'

'While we were running around, the culprit was inches away from your dozy body all the time? Is that what happened?'

'Yes, that's about right.'

'Doesn't seem to be quality leadership does it, Clarence? I told you, when we first met, I wanted you to be a leading light. Direct this relief team from the front. I wanted you to show initiative. Demonstrate some spunk. But apparently, you preferred to take a nap...'

'That's not fair, sir. I was involved in the foot-chase.'

'Well anyway. Paddy Gallaher tells me you are doing *quite well*. He seems to like you, and that means something. He says you are keen to get stuck-in. And, even though I have not seen much evidence of that myself, I trust and respect Paddy's opinion. His experience and judgement is what counts. If Paddy thinks you're okay, then I suppose you must be okay. So, I will leave things for now. Mind you, I want results. Do I make myself clear? I want the team back under your command. It's not Ruff's team. It's mine. Hear me? It's my team and I want him sorted...'

'Yes sir.'

'I want him properly stitched up, got it?'

'Yes, I've got it guv'nor.'

'What is the time on your kettle?' he asked.

'Just after midnight.'

With that, our discussion was over — the red lights started to flash on the machine — then the bells began to ring.

Inspector Beedi bent down to read the printer message:

+++ J BELLS TESTING +++

34

After I had a quick cup of tea in the canteen-kitchen, the oldest-swinger-in-town — Constable Godfrey Lambert — said he wanted to have a confidential chat. So, we went into the yard outside so he could smoke his pipe and enjoy some privacy. 'Skipper. The situation is this: I have been driving the wireless car for seven months constant. I can't go on this way... We need to get one of our youngsters trained up to 'Advanced Level' driver so I can have a rest. I fancy punting the divisional 'Q boat' around for a bit. Or perhaps driving a Panda occasionally. It's a stressful role, you know, punting the Rover around, day-in-day-out...'

'Yes. I noticed you are the only advanced driver,' I told him. 'What do you suggest?'

'You need to speak to Inspector Beedi. Get him to send one of our van drivers to the Advanced Car Wing at Hendon. It has to be a class four, van driver, of course, Sarge...'

'Yes, of course.'

'Oh, Sergeant?'

'Mmm?'

'Make it quick, though. I'm on animal leave next month. Two weeks in Torremolinos with the new wife and her sprog bin-lids. You will need to fill the vacancy pronto.'

'Yes, I see your point.'

I walked back to the station to talk over the problem with Inspector Beedi. I lurked near his office to rehearse my lines. As I approached his door, ready to negotiate, I heard a strange reedy sound leaking from within.

I rapped twice and waited for the 'headmaster' to allow me to 'enter.' The wheezy noises continued so I assumed he didn't hear my knocking over the din. I pushed the door prudently and peered into the darkened room. I saw Inspector Beedi on the far side. He had a large contraption strapped to his chest. At first, I did not recognize this *thingamajig* so I entered fully into his office to get a proper look. I'm no expert — but I think he was fingering a piano accordion. He cradled a vast squeezebox with piano-style keys on one side and a group of buttons on the other. Beedi seemed wrapped up in it — his face a picture of emotional concentration.

'Ahem.' I cleared my throat. 'Sorry to bother guv'nor. I wondered if I might have a word? If you're busy I can come back...'

The Inspector regarded me with an expression of surprise. He allowed his accordion to exhale a farty wail. 'What is it?' he snapped.

'You want me to come back?' I asked.

'No, no. I am just having a little practice. I plan to deliver a short recital at my Rotary Club dinner-dance next week. Brushing-up my skills, as it were.'

'Nice organ.' I commented.

'Hmm.' He unbuckled the instrument and placed it onto his desk with care.

'It's about our drivers.' I announced. 'We don't have sufficient Advanced Drivers on the team and poor old Godfrey can't be expected to drive the wireless car endlessly, month-on-month. He needs time out. I want to suggest we send a couple of people to Hendon. Get them trained to Advanced Level so Godfrey can have a break.'

'It should be a van driver we send,' Beedi said, rubbing his chin..

'And I would have to organize it, of course. It will require lots of paperwork. I shall have to discuss it with the Ops Chief Inspector.'

'I don't mind helping with paperwork. Or seeing the big boss, if necessary.'

'Well, I suppose it must be done. Who did you have in mind?'

'Well, as you say — it needs to be a van driver. So basically, it can only be either Ruff or Dave Yale.'

'No, no. That won't do. Not at all. I'm not having either of those renegades cowboys shooting around my patch in an area car.'

'Well, they're the only van drivers we have …' I explained. 'So, it must be either or both. I think we ought to send both.'

'Let me think it over. Leave it with me. I'll get back to you.'

'Yes sir.'

With that, Inspector Beedi waved me out of his office and picked up his giant concertina once more. As I paced down the corridor, I heard screechy sounds coming from the fun-bag: 'Sounds like a tom-cat with his dice caught in a vice,' I said to myself.

35

Most of the lads take it slow on their last shift of night duty.

And there's a good reason for that kind of lackadaisical attitude. On Monday afternoon, uniformed officers are expected to quickly switch to late turn from the previous (Sunday) night. This excruciating circumstance is known as *quick* changeover. The late shift begins at 2 p.m. And, don't forget, we completed our night shift at 6 o'clock the same day. It doesn't take a genius to figure out that you can't possibly fit adequate sleep into your cycle. So most of us don't even try to sleep. Our internal clocks are smashed anyway, so what's the point? After a week of nights, and a day that includes a quick turnaround, a policeman's stomach feels heavier than a loaded butter-churn on a cross-channel ferry. The head feels dizzy and the joints groan in protest. Then all your thought patterns become disconnected. And we feel like wireless puppets, in other words: bafflingly lanky and very run down, which is why we're probably known in the business as: Woodentops.

Apparently, it never improves. No matter how much time you spend in the Job, you never get used to a quick changeover. Older guys, like Godfrey Lambert, had done this rotation for over twenty years; and everyone of them says they feel as bad now as they ever did. So, we take it easy on the last night of the shift.

Many of us attended court on Monday morning anyway. By ten o'clock that same day, most of us will have completed 24 hours of duty. That's hard to believe, isn't it? And medical students moan about extended hours: they should try copper's shifts!

So, almost everyone attends Magistrates Court on Monday morning, after nights, the first quick changeover day on the rota. All the officers are busy over the weekend, well, maybe except for the assholes who live in the office and are bone idle, such as Inspector Beedi and Fart'n Mart'n. After all the nicking and charging at the weekend, there are lots of 'bodies' waiting in the court on Monday morning. Some of the prisoners, you could say 'the unfortunate' —it depends on your viewpoint —had been detained in police cells since Friday.

Like most quick-change teams across the Met, our relief team meets at Magistrates Court at 9:30 a.m. If an officer is lucky and has a brave disposition, he might find a cup of tea and a slice of toast with the matron. She resides in a room no larger than a wardrobe, in the cells. But the matron has her favourites, and Ruff is her darling. Matron hears his laments, makes him hot tea, passes him burned toast and adores his attention.

Others less fortunate, like young Constable Peter Prince and me, must wait around on hard benches in the public area.

So on Monday morning, Peter and I swallowed the atmosphere at Magistrates Court. The place smelled of floor polish, shoeshine and flatulence. 'What have you got?' I asked Peter.

'Criminal damage Sarge. The lad threw a beer-mug through a pub window.'

'Will he plead guilty?'

'He says *not*. I think it's pretty straight forward, though. I don't know what his defence might be.'

'You saw him throw the beer mug?'

'More or less.'

'What do you mean, more or less? Did you see it, or didn't you? Which hand did he use to throw the glass?'

'Er?'

'It's that kind of shit that might get your case thrown out, Peter.

Make sure you put in as much detail as possible. Expect to explain *exactly* what you saw.'

Constable Prince flicked nervously through his I.R.B. notebook. He found a page of notes and began to read them over. I saw fresh beads of perspiration on his forehead. His hands wobbled. 'It's a game,' I suggested. 'Some you win, some you lose. You learn as you go along. You'll be fine.'

'Thanks, Sarge,' he said. But I knew he wasn't listening.

Shortly after that, I saw Ruff approach, with Dave in tow. They advanced quickly and confidently. Dave munched a slice of Sunblest toast that he must've grabbed from the court matron.

'Alright, son? What news from Cadbury?' Ruff asked, directing the question to young Peter Prince.

P.C. Prince regarded the overawing figure of the senior Constable.

'I've got a tricky one,' he replied. 'The geezer I nicked for Crim Dam at the weekend. He wants to go for trial.'

'Let's look at your notes,' said Ruff. 'I'm sure everything will be fine. Let's have a butchers anyway — see if you left anything out of vital importance...'

'Thanks, Ruff, that's good of you. I appreciate your advice.'

Ruff took the young Constable's I.R.B. notebook and wandered off.

'Good of him,' the young Constable remarked, as Ruff passed from view and into the thick of the crowd.

In a little while the court ushers, those grizzled list-callers you get at all London magistrates, emerged from holes to start shouting-out names. Once they'd successfully gathered all the defendants around their doors, they begun to roll-call officers. The usher for Court One called for 'Constable Peter Prince' so I went with him to the courtroom door.

'Constable Prince?' questioned the shrivelled man, holding a clipboard. The guy dragged on a thin Woodbine before he coughed up a splodge of saliva. He spat it onto the morning list. 'Bollocks,' he grumbled, as he brushed the greenish phlegm away with his cuff.

'Yes, Constable Prince present.,' Peter told him.

'Good. You'll be first on. Nice little trial.'

107

'Has he entered a plea?'

'I already told you, sonny, didn't I? Nice little trial.'

A lady lawyer approached. She wore a blue hat and smelled of lavender. The wrinkled usher suddenly seemed more interested in her than us. 'Can I help you love?' he said, as he sucked-in his beer-gut. The fragrant lawyer commenced a long and detailed discourse about a committal hearing she wanted to list. They ignored us, so Peter and I slipped back to our shiny bench, though by now our place had been taken over by a large buttocked woman who wore a flowery dress. The floor had been littered by her shopping bags. The court-house had filled up nicely.

'Where the fuck is Ruff?' blurted constable Prince. He'd only just realized Ruff hadn't returned with his notes. His hands shook, and his eyes became agitated. 'I cannot see him in the crowd. He still has my I.R.B. notes'

'He's around, don't fret,' I said.

'He's got my notes. I am about to go into court. I'm literally fucked without those...'

'No need to worry. Not just yet. They'll have the over-nighters up before the beak *first*. There'll be six down in the cells. After that, they'll hear the applications. That nice lady will ask for a committal, which will take at least 20 minutes. It will be a half-hour before you are called —'

As I uttered those immortal words, the usher shouted: 'Constable Peter Prince.' We both glanced at the old git in surprise. The court official gazed back and seemed prickly.

We stepped back to him and stood in his presence while he growled with displeasure. 'Where the fuck did you get?' he snapped. 'I told you to be ready. I warned you that you'd be *first on*. Why'd you walk away? Do not be such a dipstick, son. The whole court is waiting for you.'

'I'm sorry,' constable Prince said. He scanned the bustling building once more, in the earnest hope of seeing Ruff who'd gone missing with his notes. But the usher gave such an exasperated look that it seemed dangerous to wait any longer.

'Get in there, boy,' shouted the usher. 'The magistrates are waiting. God help me...'

Peter Prince opened the massive doors and half-heartedly crossed the threshold of the courtroom. Just in the nick of time, Ruff appeared from nowhere. 'Here you go, young man,' he said, with a rosy smile. 'You almost forgot your notes.' He pushed the precious I.R.B. notebook into Peter Prince's sweaty hands.

'Thanks, Ruff. Crikey, that was a close one,' Peter muttered before he let rip an enormous fart.

'*Hmm,* made to make your mouth water,' Ruff said with a wink.

We shuffled into court behind young Peter and went to sit in the public gallery. There wasn't enough room for us to all sit on the wooden benches, so Ruff crouched to one side. The clerk-of-the-court peered at us from his silver-framed bifocals: 'If we can begin, please? Are some of you officers witnesses in this case?'

'No, your worships,' shouted Ruff, loud as a bell.

'Well, can you be quiet, please? We're trying to get this started. We are running late already as it happens... due to the officer in the case being late...'

After that, the charge was read to the defendant, who seemed to be one of those flashy confrontational types. Peter Prince was asked to take the witness stand. He wandered into the box and gave the 'audience' a nervous look. Ruff gave him an encouraging thumbs-up sign. So the young Constable introduced himself and took the oath. After that, he said, 'May I refer to my notes your worships?'

'When were they made?' asked the chairman.

'They were made shortly after the incident and fresh in my memory,' Peter replied, as he had been trained. The magistrates glanced at each other and seemed to agree it would be okay if he looked at his notebook.

'Yes, you may refresh your memory with your notes,' said the chairman. 'Please proceed. And get on with it officer. We have a long list to get to through today, and we're already late, no thanks to you...'

Constable Prince cleared his throat and opened his I.R.B. to the essential pages of the notebook: the details of the evidence. He looked blankly at these pages, and I'm sure I saw his face turn white.

He glanced at the Justices, who sat across from the sour-faced Clerk and looked exasperated. He turned his head towards the irascible old usher who looked at him with an expression that verged on homicidal. Finally, the penny dropped, and he gazed at Ruff. Without a sound, but clear to see, he mouthed: 'You fucker.'

Ruff beamed with pleasure. And he started to snigger.

Constable Prince put his notebook down and started to relay the facts from memory. He retold the tale of the man who threw a beer-mug through a pub window. His performance was highly effective. When the defence lawyer was asked, 'Does your client have any questions of the officer?' The defendant whispered into the legal ear of his advisor and shook his head. The Magistrates looked on with interest.

'Your worships. My client has decided, on the strength of that persuasive evidence to change his plea and enter one of guilty. I am grateful for your patience and your forbearance.'

'Guilty?'

'Yes, sir. The officer's evidence is compelling.'

The court was satisfied with this turn of events because it accelerated things. In fact, so happy were the lay-Justices after this surprise guilty plea, they let the man off with a discharge. And they smiled at, knowing they would now be participating in golf games, tea appointments and other middle-class activities all afternoon.

Outside the court, I found Constable Prince hiding in the crowd. I asked him what had happened in the witness box. Why hadn't he used his notes?

'Look at this...' he said. He passed me his I.R.B. notebook. I flipped through the pages until I came to the centre-fold. That's where the important 'details of evidence' notes are *typically* found.

However, written in large letters on *newly* inserted sheets were the following words:

'Peter is a little dick. His fleece so white and merry / I followed him into court today / to see him break his cherry/ it made the others laugh you see / to see his young dick pulled / He nearly bust his dirty-ring / and that's what I call fooled.'

I flipped through the other pages. Peter's original notes had been replaced by balderdash.

'The bastard.' I exclaimed. 'Mind you; I think you provided better evidence *without* your notes. So maybe Ruff helped you.'

Ruff appeared from the gent's bog and wobbled over. He gave a diffident smile.

'You wankerish spunk-monk,' Peter said. He gave the senior Constable his ugliest stare.

'Let that be a lesson to you, young 'un' Ruff said. 'Never give your notes to someone else. Keep 'em in your sweaty Germans like they're your frank and beans. They are the most valuable asset you have.'

'Ruff's right, I suppose,' I said with a sigh. 'But he's a bastard all the same.'

36

Fisticuffs and the Pitch and Toss

'So, what's the beef between you and Beedi?'

I decided to get to the heart of the matter with Ruff. I wanted to find-out what had been the root-cause of bad-blood between him and the Inspector. Ruff pulled the little Morris Minor out of the station yard. It was quick-changeover day and I was part-way through the 24-hour long shift. My eyelids flickered as we drove into the dazzling afternoon sun. My head felt like a bag of foam and my bowels frothed and bubbled like an overripe fermentation barrel.

'It probably dates to the cones —' Ruff responded. He issued a long and *very* grotesque raspberry tart. He gave a brief glance as we continued into Viscount Avenue.

'Cones?' I asked.

'Yes, traffic cones.'

'Tell me more.'

'Beedi had recently moved over here from Barnet sub-division. He was already an Inspector. I do not know the reason for his transfer, but I guess he'd had a bust-up with one of the other guv'nors. It was his first week at Quebec Mike.' Ruff paused the story so that a kindly old lady might cross the road with a heavy basket. Once she was safely over though, the old woman frowned at our Police Panda as if we were scum. Then she gave us the finger.

'Charming that is,' exclaimed Ruff. He wound the window down with crazy energy. 'Don't ye knock it all back at once, ye crazy old witch,' he yelled.

'Cock your ass,' the elderly woman replied and did the 'V' sign.

'Anyway, back to the story,' Ruff continued. He lit a B&H to satisfy his nerves. His squidgy pink fingers trembled at the wheel and his piggy eyes were more inflamed than usual. 'Inspector Beedi was new. Midweek, there was a big traffic accident along the Ascot Road. A pikey truck avoided side-swiping a cyclist, but the truck crashed into three shop fronts instead. It pulled down a pile of scaffolding. No one was hurt, thank God. But the road was a bloody mess. The store owners were understandably pissed. Some Pandas were sent to pacify the traders and take statements. And to do general things like take fucking control and keep the peace. The new Supervisor, this idiot from Barnet called Mr. Beedi decided to participate. He wanted to *supervise* the occurrence. Probably thought the accident was a major incident or something.'

'Where do the cones come into the story?'

'I am getting to that...' Ruff said. He blew a cloud of smoke across the front seat. 'So, I was there. I waved my arms about. I chatted to witnesses. I assessed the situation — as it were. And then this Inspector Beedi fella came over to me and he said: There's a stack of traffic cones by the scaffolding. Put them out for me... Cordon the area off...'

'And?'

'And? And I looked at him as if he had gone Radio Rental. I said to him: I aren't fuckin' doing it. Get the council to do it —'

'He didn't like you fronting him up?'

'It got worse than that...' I tutted under my breath. Ruff always made life difficult for himself. Weaker officers yielded to institutional expectations. But during the last few days I'd learnt that Ruff fancied himself as the lone voice of reason. So, he took another drag on his ciggie and said, 'Beedi said: *It's a direct order. I'm not going to repeat it. Get over there and grab the cones and put them out. Before I stick you on.* So I said: guv'nor — I am not doing it. It's not a copper's job. My uniform will get shitted. I will put my back out. I will strain myself and get a hernia. What's the point anyway? Call the Council and get them to put the ruddy cones out if you *really* think you need them. Then Beedi gazed at me as if I was a pile of shitnuggets and said: *Go over there and get the ruddy cones out.* I gazed at him truculently and said: shan't. Then gave him a wink.'

'Wink? Why did you give him a wink?'

'To defuse the situation. I suppose.'

'Did the wink help?'

'No. It made matters worse. I think it was the wink that maddened him. He rushed over to the other guys. He told them to get closer. I went to have a gander...'

'What did he tell the other guys?'

'He said he wanted everyone to grab the dirty cones and put them out. Incidentally, Skipper, the cones were about four-feet high. And weighed as much as a sack of fucking coal. I do not want you thinking I was making a mountain out of a molehill. Right? These were giant ruddy cones...'

'Okay, yes. Go ahead with the story.'

'So, the lads looked at me. As if I was the boss, like...'

'I see.'

'And then my mate — Dave — he ignored what the new guv'nor had said, and instead turned to me and went: *What do you think Ruff? Inspector* Beedi went mad when he heard that. The inspector screamed. He said: *Do not ask the Constable what he thinks. Just get the cones out. Am I going crazy? Why doesn't anyone listen to me?*'

'What did you tell the lads?'

'I told them that I didn't think it was our job to put cones out. I told them I thought it was the council's job. I told them I wouldn't be doing it.'

I nodded. Ruff pulled the Panda into a parking spot near the newsagent. He opened the door of the little motor.

'Don't leave the story dangling Ruff. What happened next?'

'That's it. The end of the story.'

'The end?'

'Yep. We *didn't* put the cones out. None of us. The council came and did it like I suggested all along. We completed an accident report. We nicked the pikey on a trumped-up charge. Then we came back to the canteen and had a long break.'

'Didn't the Inspector stick you on? Didn't he threaten you or even give you a pocketbook caution?'

'No. He never said another word about the incident.'

'But it's played on his mind ever since?'

'Probably.' My bowels churned. My head started to throb. Clearly, I'd been damaged by the quick-change-over and a general lack of sleep.' Want something sweet?' Ruff asked. 'I'm going to buy twenty B&H and get *something* that helps recovery.' He pointed towards the newsagent.

'Yes. Thanks.'

Ruff slammed the car-door shut. The impact caused my bones to shake and my head to resonate like a cheap banjo.

In a bit Ruff returned to our Morris. He held a gold cigarette packet in one hand and a Cadbury's Bar Six in the other. He threw the chocolate bar to me: 'Get that inside you.' Then he revealed a dark green bottle of Q.C. Cream Sherry from his inside pocket. 'Take a swig of this too. It will do the world of good. It's a tonic. Restorative wine.'

I gazed at the unopened bottle. My aunt took Wincarnis daily so I knew it that fortified wine could be effective. But officers were not permitted to drink on duty, let alone purchase alcohol.

'You've just bought this?' I asked.

'Yes. Over there.' Ruff indicated the off-licence. It was attached to the Crown public house. 'I got Dee-for-Pee. They know me in there. They don't mind me going in...'

'For the love of Christ, Ruff...'

I unscrewed the cap and glugged down a mouthful. I admit the liquor tasted agreeable. Slightly oily but smooth.

Ruff checked my reaction and approved. Then he grabbed the bottle and took a swig himself.

'I thought you was off to get Lucozade.' I commented.

'This is better.' Ruff said, before belching and handing back the bottle. 'Right. Let's go. Things to do. Places to go. People to see.'

The Morris Minor roared into life and we thundered down the street with renewed vigour.

37

A little while later we heard a call from Quebec Mike.

A civil trespass at the shops in Park Drive. Apparently, an ex-employee had barged into the sports equipment shop in the Crescent and demanded his back-pay. The manager of the store had called for police to attend and eject the character.

Fart'n Mart'n responded to the call: 'Yes, I will attend that. I was about to do a background check on a dumped vehicle, but I'll divert to that instead. Show me assigned.'

'That's a fairly typical job for Fart'n Mart'n,' Ruff explained. 'He loves that type of call. No stress, no conflict. No arrests. It will take hours to complete. Half a day to write a fucking report. Lazy bastard...'

'Do you want to go?' I asked.

'Nah. Let's go look around the park. There might be a bit of crumpet strolling about.'

So, we headed to the kids playground. In fact, we were about to squeeze the Panda through a pair of rusty gates when we heard the guv'nor call-up on the bat-phone.

'I am nearby that trespass call too,' the guv'nor transmitted. 'I will attend also.'

Ruff steered our tiny Panda around the children's pool. There was a marked absence of any crumpet. I spied an old vagrant on a park bench who sat in a pool of his own piss.

'Where's the crumpet Ruff?' I asked.

'Shhh,' he said abruptly. 'What was that?'

I didn't hear a thing.

Ruff held his talking-brooch close to his ear. I wondered if this was another wind-up. Another laugh at my expense. But, no, judging by the serious expression on his face something was very definitely *wrong*. Suddenly he slammed the brakes on and made an extravagant U-turn.

Then I heard it. Crackle, crackle hiss. Nothing more. Just that. Crackle, crackle hiss, hiss.

I knew what the sound meant. It was one of those things you came to recognize with experience. Muffled it might have been, but the hairs on the back of my neck stood on end and my stomach grumbled. The sound meant trouble. I did not dare say another thing. I even tried to keep my breathing down. I held my talking-brooch close to my ear.

Ruff took the Panda out of the park then drove proficiently, but *very* swiftly, down the main road. All the while he focused on the sound — or lack of it — that was coming from the bat-phone. Crackle, crackle hiss.

'Zeh. Shtteh. Preddz...' The call was being made from Fart'n Mart'n's bat-phone. He'd uttered something entirely unintelligible. The signal had been totally disrupted by static. I couldn't understand a bloody word.

'All units. From four-one-three...' shouted Ruff, suddenly. Somehow, don't ask me how, Ruff had managed to interpret the message: 'Get to Park Drive on the hurry up — Fart'n Mart'n is in trouble. Needs back up. I repeat. All units. All units. Park Drive on the hurry-up. Officer calling for urgent assistance.'

Units began to respond. 'Quebec Mike from four-one-three?'

'Go ahead Ruff.'

'Can you raise Quebec Mike one? The duty officer said he was going to attend this call as well, haven't heard from him yet —'

'Roger that. Quebec Whiskey One, Quebec Whiskey One. Are you receiving over?'

There was no answer.

'No reply, Ruff.'

'Noted. All units. Keep radio traffic to a minimum. First unit on scene provide an update. I repeat. Keep radio traffic to a minimum until someone has an update. Out to you...' Ruff communicated this message swift and effectively. I must admit that Ruff thought faster than me.

It went quiet after that. Everyone followed Ruff's instructions.

We were about sixty seconds away when we heard Fart'n Mart'n's voice on the bat-phone.

'Quebec Mike, Quebec Mike from one-twenty,' he said, quite nonchalantly as a matter-of-fact. His transmission possessed an unexpected air of calm.

'Go ahead. Are you okay? We thought you were asking for urgent assistance. You weren't responding...'

'Yes Quebec Mike. I am fine. I am at Park Drive dealing with a civil trespass. A male suspect has made off from the scene description as follows: Male RC1, about six feet tall and wearing a blue tracksuit. He is carrying a blue sports bag. Inspector Beedi has been assaulted. I repeat, the Inspector has been assaulted. Ambulance required. Plus, one unit to the scene to assist me with the report. And search for missing suspect.'

'One twenty. Did you say the duty officer has been assaulted?'

'Yup.'

'Is there a request for an ambulance?'

There was another pause. As if Fart'n Mart'n asked the Inspector if he needed to go to hospital.

'No *cancel*, the inspector says he does not need an ambulance.'

We rumbled into Park Drive and came to a hand-brake-stop outside the sports shop. I saw Inspector Beedi. The boss held his cheek. I saw blood on his face. At the Inspector's side was Fart'n Mart'n. The Constable had his hands on his hips, like he usual, and his cap tilted onto the back of his head. He stared into space with misty indifference.

Ruff and I jumped out of our Morris Panda car and I went to see Fart'n Mart'n while Ruff approached the guv'nor.

'Are you OK?' I asked Mart'n.

'Oh yeah, fine. The Inspector got a knock though.'

'What happened?'

'The Inspector arrived before me. He stepped over to the shop and confronted the suspect. The fella side-stroked him with a sports bag.' I glanced at the store and saw a man aged about forty years standing by the entrance. He had a thin blue tie, greasy yellow collar and wore shiny trousers. He had an expression that seemed to be a mix of concern and anxiety. I supposed he must be the manager of the shop.

'You had a good look at the suspect?' Ruff asked, abruptly.

'What, me?' Fart'n Mart'n said.

'Yes, of course *you* Fart'n. Who do you ruddy think? Snow fucking White? The guv'nor can't exactly be a witness to his own assault, can he? Anyway, he's been hit in the snotter so a good brief will get the suspect off by suggesting the boss couldn't possibly identify an assailant due to a runny nose and bleary eyes. He's no good as a witness anyhow. So, yes, that's why I'm asking *you* — did you get a good look at the suspect?'

'Well yeah. I put out the description on my personal radio, didn't I?'

'I heard that. Which way did the fucker go?'

Fart'n Mart'n pointed across the road towards a back alley that led to detached garages.

'Didn't you think to chase after the fucker then? To nick him?'

'I wanted to ensure the Inspector was in good shape. I was tending him.'

'Tending him huh?' Ruff made a tutting noise. By then other units started to arrive. I ought to have given everyone an update: in the excitement I had forgotten.

Dave came to our position. 'Dave, follow us in the van...' Ruff told him, 'We need to nick the tosser who did this. He's down that alley.'

'Sure.'

'Come with us Fart'n,' Ruff directed.

'My Panda is over there,' Fart'n Mart'n appealed. 'I can drive over *later* if you want.'

'Oh no you don't. We're wise to your lily-livered fuckery,' Ruff said, with a firm grasp on Fart'n's arm. 'I know you, once inside your nice warm Panda, you'll lock the doors and put your head up your arse. I'm not having that... you will jump in with us and we'll do this *together*. Let's go.'

Ruff *physically* guided Fart'n Mart'n towards our Morris Minor.

'Jump in.' Ruff indicated to me. He wanted me to get into the back. I gave a blank look but did as I was told. Fart'n Mart'n got in the front of the car with Ruff who fired up the little motor. We lurched across the main road and rambled down an alleyway that led to the garages. Halfway down the clinker lane we spotted the suspect. He seemed tall and agile. He walked slowly. He held a sports bag in his left hand. The Panda tyres crackled on the cinder surface as we briskly approached.

We scraped to a stop just inches from the suspect's legs. In fact, in all honesty, I thought that Ruff might run him down.

'What?' I could hear the man shout. 'What do you want with me copper?' He waved his arms in annoyance.

'Stand still' shouted Ruff.

'Get out...' I said to Fart'n Mart'n. 'We need to back-up our colleague.'

'He seems okay — ' Fart'n Mart'n announced calmly. 'I think Ruff can handle this. We might as well stay put...'

So, I found myself stuck behind Fart'n, who refused to budge his seat: 'Don't be rifuckulous...' I shouted. 'This asshole has already twatted a copper. He's shown he's dangerous and needs to be sorted.'

I saw Ruff go for the man's sports bag. On impulse, the suspect snatched it away — but he wasn't quite fast enough.

All this while, Fart'n Mart'n refused to unroll his body from the Panda. In fact, he gave a long sigh as if he had all the time in the world. I watched as Ruff pulled on the handle of the suspect's sports bag with all his strength and the man had release his grip to avoid being hauled over. 'That's mine, that's mine. Fuck you. Give it back, give it back —' shouted the man. Ruff took the bag and slung it behind him, onto a patch of wet nettles.

'If you want it — you better go get it...' Ruff said. He gave the man one of his legendary winks.

The man seemed riled by this. He started to move as fast as he could, to retrieve his bag. That's when I made my own move and climbed over the driver's seat that had just been vacated by Ruff and launched myself head-first through the door of the Morris. I tumbled onto the dust-road and smashed my knee as I collapsed. But at least I was out of the Panda. As I got up, I rubbed my limbs and looked back at Fart'n who was still sat in the car. Then I watched the suspect bend down to grab his sports bag. I also witnessed Ruff assault the man: he kicked him soundly and accurately in the balls.

The suspect dropped like a sack of coal.

'Not so big *now* — are you?' Ruff said. The man groaned as he rolled on the gravel. 'The pint that thinks he's a quart...'

I heard crunching noises behind. The van pulled in.

No that the suspect had been rendered safe, Fart'n Mart'n managed to drag himself from the police vehicle. He composed himself in the alleyway and assumed his normal stance. With that look of stupid indifference on his plain face and his cap on the back of his head, hands on his hips.

'Better late than never, I suppose.' Ruff commented. Then he grabbed a handful of the suspect's hair and pulled his face up so we could all have a good look. 'Here's *your* prisoner Fart'n. Do you want to go over Judges Rules with him? Or do you want to sling him straight into the back of the van? '

'My prisoner?' Fart'n Mart'n exclaimed. He was *incredibly surprised* by this news. 'I thought you'd nicked him, Ruff...'

'It's your call Fart'n. I'll take him in if that's what you want. But you might get done for neglect if you don't nick him. Only saying... Why did you let him get away? Why did you let him slip off? That's what A.10 will ask when they start their enquiry into neglect-of-duty. They'll probably conclude the Inspector could have been looked after by the shop manager. They will also conclude that you bottled it. And that's why you didn't go after him....'

'I waited for reinforcements,' Fart'n Mart'n explained. 'That's the correct procedure. Isn't it, Sarge?'

'Don't bring me into it,' I told him. I hated it when the constables did that. 'Ruff is right,' I continued, 'It's *your* body. Good and fair. You'd better get him in the van pronto. And you'll not get done for neglect...'

Fart'n Mart'n sighed and approached the suspect. The man was, clearly, still in some pain, I could tell by the grimace on his face. The fight had been taken out of him by Ruff's swift kick to the bollocks. Fart'n Mart'n began to repeat Judges Rules.

'Go on twat him,' said Ruff, once Fart'n finished the caution: 'Twat the Berkeley Hunt, Martin. He needs a good thumping for what he done to the boss. We won't say *nothing*, will we Skip?' Ruff gazed at me. 'You can give him one down here. We're not overlooked...'

'There's no need to hurt the man —'Fart'n Mart'n said.

'Your choice...' Ruff commented.

So, we helped Fart'n Mart'n to manhandle the suspect into the back of the van. We heaved him in unceremoniously.

Fart'n Mart'n then located the discarded sports bag in the nettles and was about to throw it into the back of the van.

'What's the matter with you Fart'n?' Ruff shouted. 'Are you fucking crazy? Do NOT give *him* the fucking bag. You don't even know what's in it. Have you searched it yet?'

Fart'n shook his head.

Ruff grabbed the sports bag and placed it on the ground. He unzipped it so we all peered inside. Ruff pulled out a towel and a pair of Plimsoll shoes. Under those items we all saw a bit of rusty metal.

Ruff pulled the tarnished iron into view. It looked like a Second World War service revolver to me. We gazed at the gun in wonder.

'See? I told you *not* to give him the fucking bag,' Ruff said. He checked the chamber: 'You were *actually* going to chuck him the bag, weren't you? What a twat you are. *Hmm,* loaded too.'

When he heard this news Fart'n Mart'n crouched and his face went pale. Then he vomited his guts up. The spew landed all over the nettles.

Once we'd taken Fart'n Mart'n's prisoner to Quebec Mike, we completed our reports and two C.I.D officers came down to 'take the job over.' They were interested in the gun and wanted the man charged with firearms offences in addition to the assault. The Inspector wanted 'no fuss' and asked for 'no special treatment.' He said he would only sign the charge sheet for the least serious offence of assault on police. He told the D.I. he would not go for a charge of A.B.H.

However, he told the D.I. that he had been extremely impressed with Fart'n Mart'n and later told Sergeant Paddy Gallaher to 'write him up' for a good arrest. 'I'm not suggesting that Martin was markedly gutsy —' Beedi explained, 'I know he admitted he didn't know what was in the sports bag. All the same, he *did* subdue and restrain the prisoner before the man had recourse to use the weapon. Those facts should be declared in your report.'

There was no recognition of the role Ruff played at the scene. Perhaps that's best. But I wanted to ask Ruff how he felt: 'Are you happy with this situation Ruff? Are you glad Fart'n Mart'n got approval when, in fact, he acted like a spineless, droopy-limbed chickenshit?'

'I don't give a flying fart either way. The both of 'em are wormy fuckers. They suit each other.'

'Beedi and Fart'n Mart'n?'

'They're both from the same box, aren't they? The box marked: weary. They're both weary, work-shy, shit-for-brains.'

38

I had brought Charlie Butler into the station earlier to act as a late-turn gaoler for the police cells because things tended to get busy on the quick-changeover. He'd already dealt with a shoplifter that had been nicked on the early turn and a chap who'd been arrested on a warrant.

'The creeping insects are going to interview the son of a bitch who hammered the Inspector,' M.C. Butler told us.

'Yes, I know,' said Ruff. 'By the way — you shouldn't refer to detectives as creeping insects...'

Charlie Butler smirked: 'What should I call them Ruff? The dirt? The filth? The suits? I *have* to call them *something*...'

'No, you don't — you're not eleven years old any more. Don't call people *anything*. This isn't a fucking school playground; it's real life...'

The criticism hurt Charlie Butler. I saw him wince from the whiplash off Ruff's acid tongue. I reckon it knocked his confidence off-kilter. Charlie M.C. Butler attempted to fight back and reason-out things out: 'They're slackers though aren't they Ruff? Not like us. They don't work at the coalface. Back-room boys, aren't they? Their backsides are shiny, and they've got nothing going on upstairs. Nine to five skivers...'

With that, Ruff grabbed Constable Butler's chin and squeezed his lower lip with his large flabby-pink fingers. He gazed into the younger Constable's eyes: 'Do not name-call officers...'

'Ouch! You're hurting me, mate' Charlie Butler gurgled. Ruff held his bottom jaw and wouldn't let go. The young Constable tried to pull away, but Ruff was having none of it. He pushed Butler against the charge-room wall: 'I've had it with you, Butler. You're a nasty little fuck with a bad attitude and fewer brains than a lugworm. Stop being such an ignorant shit and grow up. Got it?' With that, Ruff pushed Butler's skull hard against the wall, and I heard the sound of bone cracked against concrete. Then he released him. I should have interrupted — I know I should have. But I admit I was interested to see where this would go...

'Ruff sorry. I'm sorry. I'm sorry, Sarge.'

'Good, that's better,' Ruff said, as he muddled the young Constable's hair as an old mucker might do. After that, he slapped the lad, good-naturedly, around the jaw. 'You're a good boy, yeah? But behave... Eh?'

'Yes, Ruff.'

'You see the fact is this: We're all in this together. Us, the suits on the C.I.D. floor, the governors above them on the top-floor, the blacks rats, the special patrol group, the dog handlers, the donkey wallopers, the noddy-bike riders, the gadgets, the hobby-bobbies, the lolly-pop ladies. Even Beedi. We are *all* family. We need to stay healthy. Stay close. The world fucking hates us — hates our family. They want us dead. That's why we have to keep close. Watch each other's backs. Don't you see that?'

'Yes, I do now. Once you explained it,' Charlie said.

'And the C.I.D. are better than us, *anyway*...'

'How do you figure that?' I interjected.

'Because they don't wear a uniform, do they? They don't have a *Colgate ring of confidence* around them like we do. Our blue uniform is a natural protective barrier. But they don't have it, do they? So, it's more difficult for them...'

'I see...'

'A lot of the lads on relief are uniform carriers. But if you haven't got a uniform, how can you be a carrier? In C'I.D, they don't have carriers...'

Charlie M.C. and I gazed at each other, then looked at Ruff. He hadn't finished: What do pissed labourers shout on Friday night? *You wouldn't be so brave if you didn't have your uniform* on they holler. And it's fucking true. How many of *our guys* would take their uniforms off and go one-on-one with a huge Irish roustabout?'

'You would,' Charlie Butler said, eager to please.

'Not many would,' continued Ruff. He ignored the empty-headed complement. 'But the guys from C.I.D. do. They do it every day. They go one-on-one with scum all the time. Because they *must*. They don't have a blue uniform to protect them.'

'But is a uniform any protection?' I had to ask. I was not clear in my mind about the point Ruff was making. 'Look at Beedi for example,' I added. 'He was clobbered, wasn't he? But he was in full uniform ...'

'That's my point, Sarge,' Ruff explained, addressing me with a squint in his eye. 'Do you think the shithead with the sports-bag would have used his gun if someone in civilian clothes had approached him?' I gazed back at the Constable. 'THINK ABOUT IT...' he bellowed. His saliva struck me in the face, and his eyes glowed crimson. 'The suspect walloped the Inspector with a sports bag, didn't he? That's all. Then ran off on his twinkle-toes. He could have done serious damage to those two weeds. But he didn't, did he? You saw the size of him. Big as a shithouse. And armed to boot. But did he do any harm to those two tossers? No. Why? Because they were in uniform. The blues that we wear make geezers like him — even tasty geezers — think twice before they strike.'

'Yes, I see,' I said quietly. The incident had severely affected Ruff.

But then, as swiftly as he'd turned to anger, he converted to cheerful again. Back to good-ole loveable Ruff. This time he muddled *my* hair and said, 'Enough of this. Let's go out and find something...' He gave me his famous half-lipped, twisted smile. Then started to jingle the Panda keys. 'See you later, M.C.' he shouted to Charlie Butler. 'Keep up the good work.'

'Aye *aye*, captain...' Constable Butler replied. 'Sarge, see you later.' He nodded to us both then went to check the prisoners.

39

I felt encouraged and pleased that Ruff was back on top form as we drove the Morris into the evening air. He cracked jokes and chatted about his old lady. We proceeded into town when a call came out over the bat-phone: 'Any unit deal with an allegation of gross indecency. At the gent's public convenience in Myrtle Grove Park.'

'Yes, we'll take a look,' Ruff replied. 'Show Panda three.' He acknowledged the call without checking with me. He sensed my disapproval and glanced over to say: 'This is alrighty, isn't it Sarge? I'm sorry, I should have asked first.'

'Fine,' I muttered, but I admit I was a little perturbed.

'Four-one-three,' said the Comms officer, 'The attendant has asked for a silent approach. The suspects are under observation.'

'Received and understood,' Ruff replied. Again, before I managed to interject. I noticed he rarely allowed me any thinking or reaction time. Maybe it was because he was so quick-witted, or perhaps (as Inspector Beedi claimed) he was just plain insubordinate. 'You do not allow me to deliver the goods...' I grumbled.

'Sargey, sorry.'

Soon enough, we arrived near the public bogs in the crappy town-centre park. Ruff turned off the engine a good thirty paces away from the toilets, so we coasted to a halt before we arrived at the 'cottage.'

Our turquoise blue Panda could not be seen through the wire mesh windows. We fussily closed our car-doors softly, then tiptoed smartly to the front door of the public convenience. A dusty looking old-timer waited to meet us, his hair speckled with dandruff and his fingers brown-stained with nicotine. The toilet attendant was dressed in brown cotton overalls. A smelly mop and tin bucket were placed clumsily by the green door — possibly in a bid to block the exit way.

The toilet cleaner spoke first: 'The dirty bastard is in there. Giving himself a hand-shandy. I thought he'd be over before you got here. So, I put the bucket over the door to bar his escape. You took your time...'

'Thank you, Grandpa. Anyone else in there?' Ruff said.

'No. One pansy is enough, isn't it? He's probably waiting for another nob-gobbler to arrive. That's why I shut the entrance. I don't want *them sort* coming and going...'

'We'll see what's going on.'

I gave Ruff an oblique look, and he shrugged a response. We stepped into the bog. Ruff told the attendant to wait outside.

Once inside the unpleasant toilet Ruff indicated that I should pull my battery pack clear of my radio. He mimed a big *shhh!* as he placed an index finger to his lips. He took two giant strides to the line of sinks and twisted all the cold taps to full power. Then he went down onto his knees. Ruff started to crawl along the piss-stained floor.

He gestured I should do the same. Begrudgingly, I went down on my knees. I felt the damp permeating the cloth.

We advanced, little by little, on all-fours and made our way to the one cubicle in the building that was *engaged*. Behind us, we heard spouting water as the taps gushed away. That sound disguised our crawl. We reached the restroom stall together, and Ruff bent his head to peek under the bottom of the door. I followed suit. I saw a man's shiny shoes and grey socks. I strained my neck a bit more and saw the same man's hairy shins. When I contorted my head further, I felt Ruff's neck-hairs close to my ear.

Finally, I managed to get a good look at the suspect.

The man had a glossy magazine rested on knobbly knees. His fingers were gripped around the cockhead of a purplish and very erect penis. It was the most grotesque thing I'd seen — or done, as it happens —in my whole life. I felt dirty and degraded by the experience. Our behaviour seemed unacceptable. *Can't a guy have a quiet Tommy Tank in peace?* I asked myself. *Why does he have to endure two uniformed policemen spying under a toilet-door at him?*

Before I could overthink things, though, Ruff stood up. He brushed his uniform down a bit, then hammered onto the cubicle door with his first: 'Come out. Come out. This is the police. Open the door this instant, or we'll put the boot in.'

I could not extricate my head from the gap under the bog-door quick enough. I saw the man drop his magazine and bend to grab his belt, to drag up his pants. I fell backwards, the palms of my hands contacting slimy, gunky liquid on the toilet floor. I did not dare imagine what the glop might be. I heard Ruff hammer again. 'I will not ask politely another time. This is the police. Open this instant. You have three seconds.'

We heard the toilet flush then the 'suspect' shuffled to his feet.

'Three — two — one —' shouted Ruff. The toilet door opened, and a tall, well-groomed man stepped out. He wore a smart suit and red tie. He had dandyish straw-coloured hair and possessed watery blue eyes.

'Can I help you officers?' he said as if he was an innocent newborn lamb and this was the most common encounter in the world.

'You'd better wash your hands matey,' Ruff said as he pushed the man toward the sinks.

'We got enough?' I asked Ruff. I gazed cynically into his eyes. I ventured that he did not know the answer because he paid no attention.

Once the man had dried his hands on the roller towel, Ruff said: 'I am arresting you, treacle-teacake, for gross indecency. You are not obliged to say anything unless you wish to do so, anything you do say may be given in evidence...'

The man nodded politely.

'What do you want to say?' Ruff asked.

'Guilty,' said the man. In his suit pocket, we found the rolled-up magazine. It contained some homo-erotic images.

'We will need to take these,' Ruff said. I hoped to God this wank-mag wouldn't be going into our *private collection* back at base. 'This is being seized as evidence.'

I took hold of the porno magazine without thinking. 'You might want to wrap the mag in a wodge of toilet paper first, Sarge,' Ruff suggested. I peered at my gooey hands. So, I went into the cubicle and wound out a large spool of paper. I encased the gay-mag in loo-paper and went over to the sinks. I scrubbed my hands extra-hard with the sliver of brown-stained toilet soap I found on the basin.

―――

We took the prisoner to Quebec Mike in the back of our Panda. The man seemed friendly, well presented, and posh. Probably university educated, I guessed, and he appeared about thirty years old.

In the charge room Ruff related the facts to Sergeant Paddy Gallaher. Constable Charlie M.C. Butler took the prisoner to Cell Four — to rest for the night. The man would be an 'over-nighter.' That meant he'd attend court in the morning — so yet another quick change-over for Ruff.

'Charlie, it's nearly nine o'clock,' Ruff said, once the man was *banged-up*. 'Go over to the canteen manager, will you? Smile nicely and get a prisoner's meal for the geezer? She's about to knock off, so apologize for the inconvenience. Explain he's only recently come in and will be staying the night.' Ruff made it sound like the prisoner was our guest at a posh bed-and-breakfast.

'Righto Ruff. Will do' Constable M.C. Butler said. He passed the cell keys to Sergeant Gallaher and rushed to the canteen before the staff went home.

―――

'So, you caught our fellow in the fairy's phone booth with his chopper in his hands, huh? The fairy-fella's masterstroke, heh?' Paddy Gallaher's eyes twinkled. I nodded. 'I bet you've had a few *grocers* up the West End haven't you lad?'

'First I have ever had...' I told him.

'Really? I thought that's how you 'C division' lads earned your bread and honey in Soho Square. Nicking woolly woofters for cross-hand boogie...'

'As I said, I have never experienced it before.'

'Makes you feel grubby doesn't it?' suggested the old Sergeant.

'Can I ask a question?' I ventured.

'Go ahead,' replied the more experienced man.

'Well, wasn't there supposed to be two of them? In the cubicle, I mean. To complete an offence of gross indecency. Shouldn't there have been two of them performing in unison? Doing it *together*, so to speak?'

'You saw his erect penis, didn't you?' Paddy asked.

'Yup' I grunted.

'He was masturbating in a public place, wasn't he?'

'Well, I guess ...'

'He was wanking. Yes or no?'

'Yup.'

'And the wanking took place in a public convenience? Yes or no?'

'Yup.'

'And another male was insulted by his behaviour? Yes or no?'

'Er?'

'You, I'm talking about *you*. You saw him masturbating, were you insulted?'

'Yup, I suppose, but...'

'Offence complete,' Paddy said, in conclusion. 'The man was masturbating in front of another male, i.e. you in a public place, i.e. in the bog in the park. That's gross indecency that is. Plain and simple. The fella will plead guilty in the morning. He knows he's done wrong. He'll get bound over to keep the peace.'

'I see.'

40

The gaoler, Charlie M.C. Butler, arrived just after out little chat with a wobbly plate of musty-smelling food and a polystyrene mug filled with warm tea.

'Take it into the cell would you,' Paddy said.

M.C. Butler took the cell keys and paced down the corridor with the prisoner's' meal. I heard him unlock the giant door to step inside: 'Dinner is served. You dirty fag,' he bawled. Then I listened to the cell door slam shut.

'Fucking mental job this is, isn't it, Sergeant?' Butler commented once he'd returned from delivering the meal.

'How do you mean?' I asked.

'One minute I am driving a Panda. The next minute I'm molly-coddling a fucking Ginger Beer. Serving him fucking dinner and whatnot. I didn't think I would be joining this mob to become a silver-service waitress to dick-shits.'

'Dull it isn't,' I told him. Kind of 'stock reply' for this kind of moan.

Ruff had returned from having a ciggie outside, and heard my last sentence: 'What are you complaining about now, Butler?'

'Nothing, Ruff, not really...' said the young Constable. He didn't fancy another degrading physical attack from the tetchy veteran.

At that moment, the cell-bell rang. We heard a commotion from Cell Four. Charlie M.C. Butler prepared to toddle off to *see* what the fuss was, but Ruff offered to go instead.

So, Ruff lumbered down the cellblock using those great strides of his, with his giant buttocks swinging and his head wobbling. And as I watched him tootle away, I knew he was the safest Copper I had ever met. He left without protest, and I noticed that both Sergeant Gallaher and Charlie M.C. Butler watched him too. Probably, they were thinking the same as me: Ruff was a great character. Beloved by all. A rare man and very valuable. He was unique in a world filled with half-men and misfits. Ruff was a champion, fit and capable, in a realm that was made-up of weak and feeble dickwads.

As if I needed any more proof of his apparent attributes, Ruff marched back to us with a plate of food — the prisoner's meal marked 'Met Police Catering' — precisely the same plate of food that had been delivered to the prisoner a few minutes earlier by Constable M.C. Butler. He held the rancid drink in his big hand: 'Did you salt this fucking grub?' he shouted.

Salting grub is age-old retribution. It's often handed out to the worst-of-the-worst. Salting has been done by gaolers far and wide for generations. They were probably doing it in Roman times. Essentially, salting works like this: prisoners are not permitted condiments in their cells. So, the man with the cell-keys has the privilege of 'flavouring' the prisoner's meals. If the gaoler likes a prisoner, then he will get a light sprinkling of salt. However, if the gaoler dislikes the prisoner, the salt will be distributed more generously over the plate. For the worst offenders — kiddie fiddlers, cop killers and the like — the food is completely covered in salt.

Ruff had directed the question to Constable Butler. Charlie M.C. who returned a weak smile, but I could tell it was phoney: 'Me? Um, yes, Ruff, mate. I gave the grub some extra tang, didn't I? That's how they like it, don't they? Gingers, I mean. They like a bit of salt on their cocks, don't they?'

Ruff took the cover from the lukewarm food-plate and held it under the nose of the young Constable. 'Well, *you* fucking eat it then.'

'No, I don't want to Ruff,' said M.C. Butler turning his nose up and pushing his head. 'I was only having a giraffe. Honestly, it's just a giggle, mate.'

Ruff tossed the plate of salted food in the charge-room bin. Then he flicked the top from the takeaway mug of tea and took a sip. 'You salted this too. You dirty Anthony Blunt...'

'That's the way *they* like it, Ruff,' pleaded Charlie Butler.

'You ignorant fucking bastard,' Ruff shouted. He squared-up to the young Constable and looked about to clobber him. But Paddy Gallaher approached them from his desk. The old skipper moved his body between the two Constables: 'Now then. *Now then*. We'll have none of that. Not in my charge room. Settle it now. Both of you. That's an order.'

The Constables looked at the grey-haired old supervisor. 'Ruff get out and take a long drag on your ciggie. Then have a swig on your bottle of sherry. Jesus, Mary, and Joseph man, you're coiled tight as a bronze serpent today. Get out. I will deal with this...' Ruff did as he was told. He left charge room, slamming the door as he stomped.

Sergeant Gallaher turned his attention to the younger Constable: 'Now what did you have to go and do that for sonny?' he said in his soft Irish way. 'You've riled Ruff, haven't you? And that's not a wise thing to do...'

I'm sure I detected tears forming in Constable Butler's eyes: 'I'm sorry Skipper. Truly I am. I didn't know it would cause problems. I salted the woofters din-dins because he's a cock-gobbler. I didn't know it would upset Ruff. Actually, I thought that it would please him, to be honest...'

'Please him?'

'Yes, he nicked the filthy grocer, didn't he? He doesn't like *homos* any more than me...'

'Ruff is upset because the man will now think *all of us* are fucked-up shit-heads. *His kind* already thinks all coppers hate them. This confirms his worse suspicions. All you've gone and done is show the man his misgivings are true. It's too late to get more grub from the canteen. So, the man is within his rights to complain.'

'Complain Sarge? What if I suggest something?'

'What?'

'What about if I offer to pay? I have a couple of quid on me. Maybe I can offer to get him chips and saveloy. I could get them in my Panda?'

'I'll go and see the prisoner and offer that as an alternative. I doubt he will be amenable, though. I expect he's none too happy. He thinks we're *all* a bunch of shits now. He knows we can't be trusted. I'll try to make him see sense...' Sergeant Gallaher wandered down the corridor to Cell Four. I heard him chatting things over with the prisoner.

A little later, he returned to see Constable Butler.

'You are a lucky man, Butler. The prisoner is *not* going to make a complaint. I talked him out of it. I convinced him that the catering staff added the salt. Thank Mother Mary he hadn't tried the tea. I offered to buy him fish and chips, and he's accepted. So, get in your Panda, right now, and grab him a fat portion of cod and a large bag chips. And do it quickly ...'

'Sarge. Thanks, Sarge. I'm sorry, Sarge.'

'Do not be such a twat in future. Think of the consequences of your actions.'

'Yes, Sarge.'

41

A Saucepan Goes Missing

Tuesday Late Turn is, by tradition, curry night — or Ruby Murray night as it's better known. This is because, once the ninth day of work is over, the lads need to go out and have some fun, get beers in and eat a plate of proper scoff. Unhappily, they don't get away from work till at least 10 p.m. — more like eleven o'clock for most of them; So, by then, all bars are closed, and bells for last orders have sounded at the Rub-A-Dubs. Where do coppers go to relax and unwind? The Ruby Murray house.

But that was for later. Right now we had one last shift to complete before a well-earned day-off. By the way, we were supposed to have *two days* rest after nights. But the powers-that-be had determined we *had to* work one of our scheduled rest days because of our critical workforce shortage. So, half the relief was expected to work That was Thursday —fortunately, none of us needed to work Wednesday unless we were doing 'overs.' Wednesday was our proper, actual day-off. So, Tuesday night, all London Coppers shouted a combined *hurrah!* And sat around the Ruby Murray table to raise a corporate glass of Pig's Ear to the Home Office fuckers who decided, in their great wisdom, that a Copper could survive on one day off after nine days on duty.

———

I went to fetch my personal radio from the bat-cage to begin my last duty of nine shifts. I strolled past Inspector Beedi who checked the duty state: 'Ah, I'm glad I saw you, Clarence. I wanted to have a quick chat.'

'Yes, sir. Here?'

'Yes. Just a quickie.' I waited while the Inspector searched for his red pen to make an over-time 'entry' onto the duty sheet. I noticed, when I glimpsed over his shoulder, that Ruff had been in court during the morning. *God, that guy must be cattle trucked.* I thought. It was Ruff's tenth day on duty. Mind you; you never heard him complaining. 'Yes. I wanted to update you regarding the relief area car driver,' continued Beedi, as he put his pen away. Today the Inspector wore his official police-issue 'ice cream' jacket — he blue blazer that's distributed to bosses when they're working permanently 'inside.' Clearly, he intended to stay indoors. No doubt his shift would be spent fooling around with his squeezebox. 'I talked to the Chief Inspector,' he resumed. 'And the Chief agrees with me that we need a new advanced car driver on our relief. Godfrey Lambert cannot go on forever...' I kept my lips buttoned, but that's *precisely* what I had told him. 'I have chosen Fart'n Mart'n for the next advanced car course. The Chief agrees with my choice and says he might be able to slot Fart'n onto the reserve list. I know it's short notice, but we need it done fast because Lambert has annual leave coming up. If we get Fart'n Mart'n on the reserve list, we won't have to wait long.'

'Fart'n Mart'n?'

'Yes, you seem surprised?'

'Well *I am* sir, I admit it.'

'Martin did a great job the other day. With that violent prisoner, I mean, he didn't know the bastard had a gun, did he? But he stopped and nicked him all the same, didn't he? That has influenced my decision...'

'I guess so.' I groaned on the inside and hoped my expression didn't give away my feelings of miserable disappointment. Fart'n Mart'n was the very *last* person on God's green earth who deserved to go on a Hendon advanced car course. Those courses were rare as rocking horse shit. They didn't come around often, and when they did, they were considered prizes. Prizes for the best. For most Bobbies, the chance of going on a Hendon Class One Car Course was their only hope of advancement. It didn't mean extra money, no, but it was considered a *de facto* promotion. It meant you'd earned your spurs. Often the Hendon Advanced Car training was the only reason lads joined the Job. And why they stuck with it. Also, from a supervisor's point of view, the wireless car, our blue Rover P6, was driven to the *most urgent* calls. It's the car that *got to the incident first* so, obviously, we needed our most reliable and most efficient officers to man it.

When I heard Beedi's suggestion, I couldn't help mumbling the phrase: 'The Job's fucked.'

'What was that, Clarence?' Beedi asked.

I *had* to say something, I really did: 'Sir, Fart'n Mart'n is only a class five standard police driver. He hasn't even completed a van course... Therefore, he's not in line for an Advanced course...'

'I am aware of that,' replied Beedi, clearly bothered by my objection to such a brilliant plan. 'I'm aware he's only a class five Panda driver. That's why I asked the Chief to get him slotted onto a last-minute van course... and he's got him one too, starting tomorrow. Fart'n Mart'n will be ready for his advanced car course when it comes up. If all goes well.'

'Righto,' I said, as brightly as I could manage. I didn't want the Inspector to guess I thought his idea was shit and that Fart'n Mart'n was a masturbatory turd-box with the brains of a scunge beetle.

―――

As I walked past Paddy Gallaher, I repeated those famous and oft-quoted words: 'The Job's fucked.'

The old sergeant studied my face and smiled: 'What's up sonny?'

'This Job.'

'Aha...'

'I wonder who first coined the phrase: The Job's fucked?' I asked.

'Legend has it that the first person to use the expression was Sir Robert Peel himself, ' Paddy told me. 'Shortly after establishing the Metropolitan Police, in the year of our Lord 1829, and on the same day he appointed the first police officer, Sir Bob wandered into his headquarters in Whitehall, stumbled over a wastebasket, got his top hat caught in a chandelier, then dropped his arse onto a priceless George the Fourth tea-service. The world's first-ever policeman rushed in to see what the commotion was about and found Sir Robert crashed in a heap, his tit-for-tat swinging in the light fitting, with his trousers around his ankles. It seems, at that point, Sir Robert uttered those immortal words: 'The Job's fucked...'

I laughed out loud. Then went to find Ruff.

Aylesbury Duck
SCOTCH WHISKY
We Don't Give One
BLENDERS & DISTILLERS,
GLASGOW & LONDON.
MADE IN SCOTLAND.

Ruff stood in the yard by the Morris Minor, smoking a fag. 'Hello Skip, what kept you?'

'Having a word with Inspector Beedi,' I told him.

'Nothing wrong, I hope?'

I braced myself before I divulged: 'The Inspector selected Fart'n Mart'n for the next Advanced Car Course.'

'Figures, I guess.' Ruff mumbled. He seemed philosophical about the news. 'Although, he's not a van driver. Shouldn't it be Dave or me? We are van drivers, and we are next in line...'

'Beedi arranged for Fart'n Mart'n to get an emergency van course. His course starts tomorrow.'

'The Job's fucked,' Ruff remarked.

'Indeed, it is.'

Before we left the yard, Ruff and I received a radio call over our batphones from the Comms officer at the nick: 'Four-one-three, are you in a position to report a misper? A school kid hasn't returned home. Reported by mother. Girl aged nine missing. I have her description if you're ready...'

'I don't require a description at this stage. Just informant details please.'

'If you're still in the yard — come and collect the info, over.'

'Received. On the way.'

Ruff stamped on his cigarette butt and shouted, 'You coming?' He'd already started pacing towards the nick before I had a chance to answer.

42

After he'd collected a carbon of the station message — and a couple of white sheets from the binder marked 'Missing Persons' — Ruff led me to the stairwell: 'There's someone I want you to meet before we go and do this missing person report. Someone who might help…'

He ran up the stairs, and I struggled to follow him at the same dizzying speed. My legs felt tired, and I was out-of-sorts after nine days of service. Ruff waited for me on the second floor, then opened a double fire door and almost hit me in the face. He pointed to a small office near the doors, and then he signalled me to enter: 'It's the lovely June Kent…' he announced: 'June … meet our new sergeant; this is Sergeant Chesterfield.' He walked over to a slender woman who sat by a typewriter and kissed her fondly on the nape of her neck.

The woman, approximately forty years old, played coolly with her pen. Her narrow fingers were elegantly manicured, and her reddish-brown hair was pulled back in a clean bun. She wore a white shirt and her tight skirt disguised well-proportioned hips. Under the desk, I glimpsed nimble legs in black stockings. From my position, holding back by the door, I smelt her exotic French scent. The vision of beauty was completed by a pair of shiny black heels. I saw that one shoe had slid provocatively from a well-formed foot. This allowed me a short peek of her tightly assembled contours and a wondrous heel and toe. June Kent was all my erotic fantasies, rolled into one. The perfect woman.

'June is one of our plonks on our Women's Unit,' said Ruff. 'She might be able to help us with that radio call.'

June gave me the once-over. I noticed she possessed pleasing hazel eyes. She gave me a sunny smile, and her white teeth glinted: 'Hello Sargey. Where've you been hiding all my life?'

'He's a stunner, isn't he June?' Ruff said, giving her a wink.

'I should cocoa. Where are you from, lover?'

I nearly couldn't answer because I felt as clumsy as a child addressed by the striking head-girl. I felt like an idiot. So, I muttered my answer, 'West End, Miss. Savile Row. C Division.'

'*Oooh!* He's a shy one. My kind of boy,' giggled the delectable June Kent.

'On the relief, we call him 'Muddy' Chesterfield. You can call him Clarence,' Ruff offered.

'Muddy?' I asked. I hadn't heard the nickname before.

'Yeah. As in he's as clear as ditchwater,' Ruff offered with a grin. I did not know if that was the truth and whether I ought to be happy or angry. *Muddy* didn't sound complimentary, to be frank. And I knew that nicknames, in general, stuck. I also knew that nicknames denoted the opposite of what they meant; so 'slim' was always the fat lad, 'chalky' was always black and 'lanky' meant short-arsed. But at least the boys on the team had given me a pet name. So, I must have been doing *something* right.

June Kent raised herself with poise and shimmied over. She maintained eye-contact as she prowled as a stripper might do. If I were a cat, I would have purred. When she was just six inches from my face, she halted. I thought she might kiss me, but no — she didn't. Instead, she snickered. Then adjusted my tie and brushed down my collars.

'*Hmm!* He's not bad. Not bad at all. Thanks for bringing him up to see me, Ruff.' I might have blushed. 'Staying for a tea lover?' she whispered in my ear.

'We can't stop, June...' said Ruff. 'We have a misper to deal with. In fact, that's why we are here. We thought you might like to come along for the ride...'

'Okay, business before pleasure, I suppose. I'll find my tit-for-tat, and we'll go for a ride in your jam.' She turned her face towards me and growled like a baby tiger. I must have given her an expression of astonishment because she snorted sharply and said: 'Oh, Ruff. I love him already. I really do. He's so innocent. We'll have lots of fun together, won't we Sargey?' She played with the knot on my tie, then sauntered off to collect her uniform hat and handbag.

Meanwhile, I found I'd temporarily lost the ability to speak.

43

On the way to Viscount Avenue, June updated Ruff about the Commissioner's plans to bring loads more lady police officers into the Met: 'Daphne — that's Commander Skillern to you — she's abolished A4. That's the women's police unit if you didn't know, Sargey...' she tapped me on the shoulder. 'Here on 'Q' division, unlike 'C' division, we are the last vestiges of the 'old' system. Last year Daphne took over personnel at C.O. The Commissioner wants gaps in manpower plugged by women. Since the law changed last year, women get equal pay, equal opportunities, equal *everything*. It couldn't have worked out better for the Met. The Home Office are rapidly pushing classes *filled* with women through Hendon. You'll be getting your allocation of plonks quite soon. This summer, no doubt.'

'What will become of you?' Ruff asked. 'What about the girls on the Women's Unit?'

'The Women's Unit is to be dissolved. I assume the plan is that we'll go downstairs and work normal shifts. That's a shame really. We don't do nights at present. I don't relish starting nights now, not at my age...' June tapped me on the shoulder again. 'All the talent and experience that's been built-up on the Women's Unit will be gone too. Our expertise at handling children and women's matters, for example. That will be gone. On the other hand, I think a lot of goodwill come out of this plan. I'm in two minds about equal opportunities, most girls are. But we're stuck with it...'

'Will *you* go onto relief?'

'I've been offered a role in the C.I.D. office. Some of the other girls are thinking of jobs at C.O. I don't think many will go downstairs to join *you lot* on shifts. But that's all by-the-by anyhow — because you will have lots of plonks working alongside. They say that one day a quarter of all police will be female. And the London Commissioner will be a woman. Mark my words.'

'God help us,' Ruff said.

'Why do you say that?' I enquired. If every woman officer were put together as perfectly as June Kent, then I'd be most happy. 'I think it will be great to have women in the workplace.'

'What? With weedy little men like Fart'n Mart'n to protect them? And fuck-twats — excuse my French, June — fuckers like Charlie M.C. Butler? Making his prejudicial comments and acting like a prick.'

'You'd be surprised how resilient ladies can be,' June commented, 'We can put up with the abuse and rudeness. We can look after ourselves.'

By then we'd arrived at Viscount Avenue. The location of the missing person's call.

44

Once we had been invited into the Viscount Avenue address, June stepped across the threshold to the lounge and scanned the jumble of photos that were scattered on the sideboard. 'Is this your hubby on your wedding day?' she asked the informant.

'Yes, I don't know what *that* has to do with my missing child. I thought you had come about that.'

'Well, yes, we have. Someone is missing?'

'God. Don't you people know anything?' the woman who'd called us seemed very terse. 'Of course, they have.'

'Who?'

The mother tut-tutted and tapped her foot to express increasing annoyance. 'Inept,' she exclaimed, to nobody. She looked askance at the ceiling.

'Who?' June asked again. The Constable smiled sweetly, her face a picture of forbearance.

'You lot. Amateurish and incompetent...'

'No, dear. *Who* has disappeared?'

'*Christ alive!* Were you not informed?'

'We would prefer if *you* told us. We're sorry if we seem disorganised today. Please tell us what happened.'

'He disappeared a while ago. That's not important. This is about my daughter. She didn't go to school today. I can't find her anywhere.'

'Your daughter?'

'Yes, *of course,* my daughter. Who do you think I'm talking about? The Queen of bloody Sheba?'

'Sorry. Please go on.'

'There's nothing else to say. The school secretary didn't know what I was talking about *neither*. I told them I sent her to school this morning. They said she never arrived. I walked around the neighbourhood — all the way to the shops. There's no sign of her. God knows where she got to. Has she been kidnapped?'

'Does she usually walk to school?' June asked, ignoring the bad vibes.

'What do you think?' the woman said with a cantankerous snarl. 'No, she bloody flies on a bloody magic carpet.'

'Most children on this borough travel to school by bus,' Ruff suggested.

'*Oh!* The big man speaks, does he? I wondered if he might be a stuffed bear. Comes across as stupid — doesn't he? No, as a matter of fact, she doesn't go by bloody bus. She *walks* to school. Like I already told you. God, don't you listen? Do you think I am made of money?'

The mother had not asked us to sit nor offered us any refreshment. She fiddled with the buttons on her easy-clean work-coat. In the background, we heard 'Slade' being played on the radio.

'You said something about your husband going missing?' June said.

'Why don't you deal with one missing person at a time?'

'It could be significant,' Ruff added. 'We need to know if the disappearance is somehow connected to the departure of your girl.'

'God. You lot waste time, don't you? Very well. He left four years ago. Never came back. Satisfied, now are you?'

'What is the name of your husband?' June asked softly.

'What does that have to do with anything?'

'How will we find him — if we don't know who to look for?'

'Look, I called *your lot* today about my daughter. If you won't me with that problem, go back to the station. Don't bother me anymore.

Endless questions. I've had enough.' With that, the woman tried ushering us from her house. I'm surprised she didn't say 'Shoo!'

'Before we go...' June said, 'We need to make notes. For our records and so on.'

'I have no time for that...'

'Well, we can't leave until we've completed a report.'

'What do you mean you cannot leave? I insist you leave this instant— I know my rights. You can't stay in my home without permission.'

'You mentioned your daughter might have been kidnapped. That is a serious allegation. We have a legal right and a moral responsibility to stay and investigate. We want to get to the bottom of the story.'

'Story? Story is it?' said the woman. Her contempt for us grew by the second. She demonstrated this with pursed lips and narrowed eyes.

'Please tell me which school your daughter attends,' June asked.

'Does it matter?'

'Show us her room.'

'Why?'

'Where are the photos of her? I can't see her photo on the mantel. Yet you have many pictures. Do you have a picture of her?'

'Get out. *Get out* all of you.'

'Do you have her schoolbooks?' Ruff chipped in.

At this point, the woman broke down. Her blood-red eyes filled with tears and long sobs interrupted frequent gasps. She fell back into a comfortable chair. Constable June Kent knelt by her feet and placed a sympathetic hand to her cheek to wipe away a tear. The specialist woman Constable stared into the woman's eyes and gave a smile of precious compassion before she said: 'Tell me all about it my love Tell me everything.'

———

The woman continued to cry, but June did not alter from her kneeling position. She stroked the mother's hand and looked into her eyes. After a few minutes, June sat on the edge of the chair and placed her arm around the woman's shoulders to comfort her. This tough and complicated woman had become, before our eyes, a broken wreck.

'There,' June said softly. 'Let it out.' A river of tears fell from the sad woman's eyes as she shook her head in despair.

'My husband died four summers ago,' she said. 'We never had children. I always wanted them. But my wonderful husband could not give me any. You see?' She glanced to Ruff to check he understood. 'This time of year — I know it's corny — but this time of the year, I create a mental image of my daughter. That's my daughter I never had. I get maudlin, you see, so I create a mental picture of my longed-for girl. Stupid, aren't I? I can even feel her presence around the place. My imaginary girl. She comes to visit. She puts my mind at rest. But this year she didn't materialize. I don't know why. I can't create her in my mind like I used to...'

'Is this the anniversary of your husband's death?' June asked.

The woman nodded.

'What's his name?'

'Jack,' she said, with a sob.

June rubbed the woman's shoulders, then tilted her head to us. 'Guys, will you do me a favour? Wait in the car. We girls need to have a chat. You two are making the place untidy.'

With these wise words, the woman smiled for the first time since we'd arrived. She started to perk up.

Ruff and I slipped quietly from the house. And he closed the front door softly behind us.

We jumped into the Panda car, and Ruff lit himself a ciggie.

'Christ almighty that was awkward...' he said.

'Poor woman,' I commented.

45

46

The Curry Night went well.

Any earlier antagonism got chased away by dangerous quantities of frosty lager and steaming plates of vindaloo. Of course, neither Fart'n Mart'n nor Inspector Beedi were present at the team gathering. But the remainder of our relief came along for the giant scoff and to celebrate the end of nine days on duty.

The next day I slept... an agitated doze. I found broken peace in my dreams and didn't rise from slumbers till way-past seven p.m. By then, I felt bizarrely hungry — so I had to go out and scoff a feast.

Thursday, I still felt cream-crackered, so I slumped around Trenchard House and made some phone calls to arrange a section house transfer. I wanted to go into the 'Q Division' single quarters known as S.Q. 28. The place where bints can be found.

When early turn Friday arrived. I got to work early, chipper and in good mental spirits. But I was surprised that I couldn't see Ruff's clapped out jam-jar in its regular parking space by the boiler-house. *It's unlike him to be late*, I thought.

I went straight to the canteen for a refreshing cuppa. That's where I found the relief team. I immediately knew something was up. Each officer seemed subdued. I perceived an unmistakable atmosphere of tension in the air. I contemplated the eyes of the Constables as they gathered around the duty-teapot. Their faces seemed possessed by curious mental rejection.

'What?' It was the only word I could think of

'Didn't you hear?' asked young Peter Prince.

'Hear? Hear what? *No*. What's up?'

'It's Ruff and Dave Yale…'

'Shit…'

'They've been badly mashed up…'

'Mashed up? What does that mean? *Mashed up?*'

'They were on late turn yesterday. Made to work an extra shift…' Godfrey Lambert explained: 'It seems they got themselves surrounded by a crowd of thugs outside the May Pole pub. They got pulled out of their Panda and given a right proper fucking hiding.'

'A proper good fucking over,' added Peter Prince.

'Pulled out?' I asked. It didn't seem possible. Ruff and Dave? Pulled from a panda. *Was this a wind-up?*

'They're both in hospital—' interrupted 'Misty' Bill Winfield. 'Down at Northwick Park.'

'In the hospital?'

The Constables nodded in unison.

'This is not a wind-up?'

'Sadly, not.'

'Oh shit…'

47

I power-walked to the front office where I found Sergeant Paddy Gallaher.

'Have you heard?' he asked.

'Yes. Do you mean about Ruff and Dave? They've been hospitalized.'

'Got surrounded by a crowd outside the May Pole. Got fucked over.'

'Yes, so I heard. Damn.'

'The C.I.D. are involved,' he went on. 'They'll get statements today. With any luck, the main suspects will be nicked by lunchtime.'

'How many were in this mob?'

'The story is about eight big boys. Aged sixteen or seventeen. Our lads got pulled through the window of the Panda...'

'So they say.'

'The boys gave our lads a right good beating. They're lucky to be alive...'

'Christ.'

I grabbed hold of Bill Winfield and asked him to whiz me down to the hospital to see Ruff and Dave.

My mind whooshed around like a star-swing at a carnival.

On the way to Northwick Park, A&E Bill and I exchanged a few polite comments but didn't talk about the beatings. When we arrived at the hospital, I asked Bill to stay with the police vehicle. I told him I'd be back in thirty minutes.

Once I got inside, I jogged along the red line in the corridor. After a two-minute dash, I arrived at their ward.

Outside the closed doors, seated on an orange plastic chair, I found Ruff's missus, Eve Palmerston. She smoked on a ciggie. She jumped up when she saw me and gave me a friendly peck on the cheek. I held her hands. They felt moist and warm. 'How long have you been here Mrs. P?' I asked.

'All night long,' she told me.

'Is he okay?' I said. 'What's his condition?'

'He's properly bruised. Ribs are broken. Nose smashed. But his noggin seems okay, so they tell me. Maybe his spleen is ruptured, they're doing tests. They're worried about his kidneys too. So, he's not yet in the clear. But could be worse...'

'Right.'

'You'll get the bastards?'

'Oh, yes. We'll get them,' I told her as I rubbed her shoulders.

'Did he tell you that he's been sleeping in the car?'

'What?'

'Did Ruff tell you that he slept in our car every night?'

'God, no. Why? Why would he do that? Why are you telling me *this* now?'

'It's about *you*, you see. The docket you're compiling. He won't admit it, but he's worried. Worried about the shit that you're trying to rake-up on him, I suppose. He comes home late. Always pissed. He stinks. Not only of cigarettes but alcohol too. He stinks of sweat, shit and vomit. I can't stand being with him. In bed, I mean...'

'Why are you telling me?'

'I told him to sleep downstairs... on the sofa. He says: If you can't stand me in the house I'll sleep in the car.'

'How long has this been going on?'

'Since you got to the station.'

I gazed into Mrs. P's eyes. She'd been crying— her eyes were bleary, and the mascara had run. But she wasn't crying now: 'This has to stop,' she said. 'Maybe *this* is a good thing.'

'A good thing?' I asked.

'Yes. Maybe this is a sign. A sign that things cannot go on. Ruff will see sense. Now, *this* has happened.'

'What do you want him to do?' I ventured.

'Our marriage is in tatters. I want him to leave this fucking Job. Get out while he still can. Come back to the Midlands. Start a new life. A safe life. Away from alcohol. Away from cigarettes. Away from accusations — away from scum...' She used a tone of voice that sounded accusing.

'I see.'

'You'll help won't you Clarence?'

'Me? What can I do?'

'You can reason with Ruff. Tell him his life is ruined. He'll listen to you. He looks up to you. Tell him the facts. Tell him to stop lying to himself. Please. Get him to go back home, back North.'

'I — er.' I didn't know quite what to say.

'You've *got* to help me...' Mrs. Palmerston whispered. 'Let me add more evidence to your dossier. So, you can nab him good and proper...'

'What?'

'I'll tell you other things. Like how he steals and cheats. That kind of stuff. It will be good evidence for you, won't it? It will bring about the end of his career here won't it?'

'Has he ever hurt you, Eve?' She shook her head. Then touched a fingertip to her cheek. 'Only once or twice. He slapped me a few times. All Northern lads do it. That's how they were brought up by their daddies. But he never punched me or done anything more serious. Maybe he will *eventually*. He's a great guy. But he comes home angry. And, as you know, he's always pissed. Sooner or later he'll clobber me. And he'll clobber me good.'

'Will you tell me if he ever lays a finger? Promise you will, Eve?'

'Yes, obviously.'

'But other than that, I do not want *you* to get involved. If you have any other evidence — I'd rather you kept it to yourself. I do not want you getting hurt.'

'But, Clarence. This *must* stop. Ruff *must* give up the Job. I do not want him to die here in London. I don't want to return to the West Midlands as a young widow on a half-pension.' Then she cried. Tears dribbled down her face. I held her in my arms, and I rocked her.

After a while, I needed to ask another question.

'Where is Dave's missus?'

'Cleo — that's Mrs. Yale. She didn't want to come.'

'Didn't want to?'

'She can't face the agony. Seeing her man crushed like this. He's already decided to return home up North, thank God. That's between you and me. He's been deciding his future these few months. Cleo said, 'If we don't leave London now, it might be too late ...'

'Cleo, is she is waiting at home?'

'Yes. She can't stand it here in casualty. Our husbands are never around. Always working. Bruised continuously, dirty, intoxicated. They never show us love or tenderness. Always too tired. That is no way to lead a life, is it? It's a prison sentence for police wives.'

'I'll go and see her. Once I have visited the lads.'

'Best you do.'

I kissed Mrs. Palmerston then clenched her hands one more time. After that, I prepared myself to go and see Ruff and Dave.

48

I stepped into the ward to see my pair of broken soldiers.

Ruff was a state. Tubes in his veins, medical dressings over every part of his body. His eyes were closed, his congealed red eyelashes stuck with gum. His face was pale pink, with visible cuts across the chin. His head was bandaged above and below. He slept.

'Hey Sargey,' Dave muttered, from an adjacent bed. I gave him my strongest and bravest smile. Then went to sit beside him.

'What you been doing?' I asked.

'Been playing with big boys, haven't we?'

'So I see.'

'Ruff got the worst of it. They were after him. I was collateral.'

'Who was it?'

'Pikeys. Local ones. From the site on the edge of our ground. I think Ruff disagreed with their leader a while ago. Not a planned attack. They saw a chance, and they took it.'

'Would you recognize them again?'

'Probably not. Ruff would. Perhaps.'

'They say you got dragged through the Panda window?'

'That's the strength of it.'

'Doesn't sound likely to me,' I said. 'There is no way Ruff would be pulled through a window. Have you seen the size of his beer-gut?'

Dave went curiously quiet. He grimaced as a cracked rib sent a bolt of pain through one side. I leant over and bent my ear down to listen because he puckered his lips: 'Ruff will not thank me for it,' he whispered 'But you ought to know the truth ...'

'What? What truth?'

'Ruff saw the pikeys assembled in the pub car park. He got out of the Panda. He confronted all eight of them. Nine in total, if you include one in the driving seat of the van. He squared up to all eight. Then he laid into them...'

'You didn't get hauled from the Panda?'

'Do not tell anyone that. It's between you and me.'

'Why lie?'

'Ruff doesn't want anyone to think he's some kind of nutter. Or worse, an insane hero. He says the story sounds better if we suggest we were surrounded and ambushed.'

'I don't get it.'

'He gave as good as he got, Sergeant. Better, frankly. He knocked the fuck out of those Pikeys. Hammered into them. They were torn apart. In the end, they were fighting for their lives. Not him. It's them who came off worse...'

'So, what are you saying? Are you suggesting Ruff provoked the attack? Was Ruff the antagonist? What if the Pikeys tell *their side* of the story?'

'The Pikeys will never admit they were fronted by a lone Copper. They'll never admit they nearly got beaten. They are a proud race and big-headed about their fighting skills. In the gypsy-world, it's not dignified to be knocked about by one man. They'll keep *shtum*. The scumbags.'

'And you? How did you come to be involved?'

'Ruff told me to stay in the car. He said he could handle it on his own. But I couldn't let him square up to eight of the fuckers, could I? So, I got out and put the boot in alongside.'

'Good for you.'

'Yes. I'm glad I helped. Maybe I evened things up. I don't know. Things might have gotten a whole lot worse if I wasn't there to back-up my old mucker.'

'Your wife, Cleo? She hasn't come, has she?'
'Who told you that? Did Eve Palmerston say?'
'Yes. Yes, she did.'
'Cleo and Eve have conspired together for weeks. They want us — me and Ruff — to leave the Job. They think this battering is the last straw. Can't blame them, really...'
'Are you going to leave?'
'Actually, I've already decided that I am. But haven't said anything to Ruff yet. I think it will break his heart. But I've got to go, you see. Sorry, Sarge. I've got to go because I must think about my wife and my future. We want to have sprogs. Sooner rather than later. But we have no money, no time together. And now *this* ...'
'You want me to bring you anything? The next time I visit?'
'You could bring me a couple of bottles of Gold Watch and two fantasy-tarts wearing hot-pants...'

———

Outside, I saw Eve Palmerston again. She dragged on another ciggie. 'He's asleep,' I told her.
'Did you chat with Dave?'
'I did.'
'Has he decided to leave?'
'No.'
Mrs. 'Ruff' waved her hand as if to discharge me. She knew it was a falsehood.
I pussyfooted down the hospital hallway, back to Constable Bill Winfield who waited in the Panda. He'd be in the staff car park near the main entrance.
I stepped into the morning air and took a giant gasp of morning freshness. I hoped it would drive away the stench of vomit and disinfectant you always got from a hospital.
'Right. Where's he got to?' I said as I stepped off the sidewalk and into the direction of the parking lot.
That's the last thing I remembered from that awful morning.
Because it's when I got hit by the ambulance.

49

The first thing I saw when I came round was Ruff's rubicund head.

His skull wobbled stupidly above my pillow. Foolishly — nonsensically, really — I thought his red face might be an orb of ectoplasm. A floating sign, perhaps, sent to tempt me into the Elysian Fields beyond. But, looking back on it, I remember was high on opiates.

'Would you look at that? The lad's eyes are opening...'

I tried to concentrate on the ruby-red blob that resembled Ruff's head. It jiggled, bobbed, and weaved. 'Keep still you fucker,' I verbalized.

That's when I heard laughter bounce around the unfamiliar room.

'He's okay,' came a voice.

'Of course, he is,' Ruff added.

Gradually, the haze cleared, and I focused on the florid complexion of Ruff's idiotic face. Shortly after this, I started to take-in information. It seemed I was in a hospital bed and had been surrounded by five or more police officers who gathered around. I sensed I was not able to move my legs. My hands and fingers worked fine, though. But I could not lift my head.

'Would you prop me up a little?' I asked Ruff. 'Lift me so I can rest back on the pillow?'

'Course I can mate.' He e hooked his giant pink-blushed hands around my neck while I felt other hands pushing and pulling pillows into place. He grunted, probably farted, then laid my head back onto the bolster. Now I saw things a whole lot better. Along with Ruff, I could make out Constable's Peter Prince, Wally West, Bill Winfield, and Godfrey Lambert. Near the door, I glimpsed Sergeant Paddy Gallaher. Everybody was there, bar Inspector Beedi (naturally) and Fart'n Mart'n.

'I thought you didn't go out of the station?' I said to Paddy Gallaher.

'Once in a while a make an exception, lad,' I heard him cackle.

'What the fuck am I doing here?'

'You got knocked over by an ambulance, sonny.'

'An ambulance?' *Oh yes.* I half-remembered now. I was leaving the front door of the hospital, and then *something* happened — something terrible. I had a distant recollection, perhaps the threat of an ambulance looming at me. But the memory faded. As if the event occurred years ago, maybe when I was a child. My brain had efficiently tucked the memory into an alcove... and didn't want me to see.

'How long have I been here?'

'You've been out for 48 hours. It's Sunday early turn.'

'Sunday?' This meant nothing to me. Even when I fully awake, I could barely tell what day of the week it was. Shift work did that to a mind. It fucked you up.

'The driver got nicked,' Ruff added.

I did not understand what that meant. So, I said nothing. I tried to come to terms with the reality of this new situation. I tried to make sense of what I was doing here in a hospital bed.

'Bill Winfield nicked him. Didn't you, boy?' Sergeant Gallaher offered.

I saw Bill nod eagerly from the other side of the private room.

'Apparently, the L.A.S. driver was pissed. Four times over the limit.'

'How?' I managed to ask.

'Good question,' Ruff said. 'Apparently, according to a medical orderly who saw the whole thing happen — the ambulance roared up the slope in reverse. The black rats said he was driving at a ferocious speed. With the back doors open. That's probably why he didn't see you and you didn't see him. You didn't stand a chance...'

'You were looking the wrong way,' Bill chipped in.

'Yes, it's not your fault,' Ruff continued, 'You looked the right way, strictly speaking. But the bastard reversed at you. Pissed you see. Plus, he'd done a fourteen-hour shift.'

'Is he okay?'

'Lost his job.'

'That's a real shame.'

'It is.'

'Where's the Inspector?'

Paddy Gallaher came forward: 'He sent *me* in his place. Says he is too busy to see you personally...'

I was tempted to say, what a bastard. But thought better of it. Gallaher would pass it back. So I said, 'Paddy. How bad is it?' I asked him because I knew the Constables wouldn't tell me straight, whereas Sergeant Gallaher *would*.

'You're fine, sonny. Badly bruised, mind. You got a shocking bang on your head. Concussion, they say. The big problem is your spine.'

'God.' I had spinal injuries. *Is that why I could not feel my feet?*

'Yes. Your backbone took a mighty thump, so it did. It's been badly jarred. But, by all accounts, it isn't broken, God be praised. Though you won't be playing First Division soccer for a while.'

'What happens now?'

'Well, you are going to be transferred to the medical centre at Hendon. Tonight, they'll make an evaluation. You will be seen by the C.M.O. My guess is they will send you down the South Coast. To the Met convalescent home.'

'You jammy bastard. You're going on vacation, courtesy of the Commissioner,' Ruff added.

'It's lovely down there,' Godfrey offered. 'I had the pleasure of two weeks sunshine 'n' sex a few years back. Did me a world of good.'

I scanned the eyes of my 'team'. They returned my gaze. I wondered what they all thought. Jammy?

'Who takes care of things while I'm out-for-the-count?' I asked.

'The Inspector made Fart'n Mart'n a temporary Acting Sergeant. That's until you get back to full duties.'

'*Shite...*'

I heard a general chuckle.

'But I thought he was going to be the next Area Car driver? ' I said. 'Is there no end to Fart'n's bloody talents?'

'You haven't heard the best yet,' said Wally West. 'Shall I tell him, Ruff?'

'Go on, mate.'

'Fart'n Mart'n failed his course van. The nob.'

'Failed his van course?' I almost shouted *yippee*. I honestly thought no one could fail that course. Two days towing followed by a couple of reversing tests around scattered cones. It seems impossible to screw-up. Only a man as useless as Fart'n Mart'n could make a fuck-up of it...' But that means... *that means...*'

'Yes, you got it, Sarge. That means Ruff will take his place on the Advanced Car Course that the Chief Inspector arranged.'

'You are shitting me?' I said.

'We shit you not. It's kosher. The Chief used his last favour with the Driving School Superintendent to masonically magic up that miracle slot for Beedi. But the idiot Fart'n Mart'n scotched their plans. So, they needed an emergency replacement and, of course, it *must* be Ruff.'

'This is great,' I said. 'Such great news.' I'd forgotten about my cattle-trucked back or even the fact I was laid out in a hospital bed: 'What about Dave Yale though?'

The Coppers gawked at each other. Then Paddy spoke: 'Dave's leaving the Job. He's decided to go back home. They can't give him an expensive course now... since he's leaving...'

'Oh. I see,' I murmured.

'Everything worked out fine,' Ruff added.

'Yes, it really did. It worked out fine,' I repeated. I heard snorts of laughter from across the ward and saw that Peter Prince sniggered so much his eyes watered.

'What's the big joke?' I shouted.

'It's just that. *It's just that...*' Peter could barely contain himself. 'It's just this whole thing is so cocked-up. Typical police humour. You are sat in a hospital bed, all fucked up. And there's that guy next to you, covered head-to-foot in bandages — he can only just stand—but despite all that, he's off to start a challenging driving course on Monday. Additionally, one of our favourite colleagues, Dave, is leaving the Job. And yet we all agree everything *worked out fine*.'

And everyone laughed at this observation with ostentatious gusto; they needed to. It's how police humour worked: it clears the air, patches-over the-all-too-obvious cracks and soothes away problems. My mood felt much improved.

I even began to snicker.

50

Twist and Twirl on the Jam

I found no sunshine 'n' sex at the Met Police convalescent home in Brighton. Merely dull days spent in therapy with a sadistic physio named George who seemed to hate me. I couldn't wait to get back to work.

Three weeks developed into a month of convalescence but, in due course, I managed to move around more-or-less painlessly. I had never been an athlete mind. Still, once I could shuffle without any help, and I could do all the exercises that the sadist assigned me — with the dash and panache he ruddy-well expected — I was provided with a rail-warrant for London and told to report to the Chief Medical Officer.

At Tintagel House, the doctor checked me over. He read the sealed letter I had been given by the merciless physio. He wrote a few notes once he'd read the letter: 'You can go back to work next week. Do you want to go onto light duties?'

Christ no. That meant hours dealing with Process reports and accidents. 'Can I go back to shifts?' I asked.

The doctor scrutinized me and hummed to himself. Then he said:

'Look, if I were not paid by the Receiver, I would say you needed a further three months recuperation. But let's be blunt: the big boss needs every pair of boots he can get. The Met is going through a manpower crisis like it's never seen before. I can offer you light duties. Or I can get you back on the streets. What do you want?'

'I want to go back on the streets.'

'So be it. But you're a fool.'

'Yes, I know sir.'

'Hmm.' The doc had expressed his opinion. I waited in the doctor's chair to be dismissed. The C.M.O. made a few more notes then examined me through his bifocal lenses.

'You still here, sergeant?'

'Sorry.'

'Get off with you. You start your first shift Monday.'

---

23 Years Old — 23 Years Old

Rasberry Tart

Scotch Whisky

Flying Raspberry & Co
11 Queen Victoria St, London E.C.
& Quality St. Leith.

51

When I arrived at Quebec Mike the following Monday, I went straight to see Inspector Beedi.

As expected, I found him in his little office — monkeying around with his precious squeeze-organ. 'I'm sorry,' I told him right away, as I burst into bis room without warning. 'Your letters of encouragement didn't reach me down there in Brighton. There must have been some problem with internal dispatch. I didn't receive any of your get-well-soon cards either.' The Inspector put down his concertina and looked discomfited. 'Mind you,' I resumed quickly, so he didn't have time to object, 'I know why I didn't get your phone calls. It's because there's only one public pay-phone booth in the convalescent home — it's tricky for well-wishers to get through...'

'That's right. *That's right*,' he replied. 'Anyway. You are *here* now. Bright-eyed and bushy-tailed I suppose?'

'Oh, yes, sir, pleased to be back on my feet.'

'Exactly.' For a moment I thought the Inspector might apologize for his woeful underperformance. But — *no*. He seemed puzzled by my sarcasm, however. We both looked around the room and shared a few moments of discomfort before he felt ready to brief me: 'Fart'n Mart'n has done a grand job in your absence,' he declared. 'He has been doing an excellent job as an acting sergeant while you've been off sick.'

'Uh-huh'

Inspector Beedi checked my eyes and my body language. 'And, as you probably know, Constable Palmerston is driving the area car. He passed the course with flying colours. He got a Class One.'

'I see.'

'And talking about Ruff. I want you to lay off him for a bit. Give him some slack ...'

'You want me to stop his close-supervision?'

'I want you to give him a bit of rope. I'm sure he will come a cropper sooner or later. And when he does, we'll act. But Paddy Gallaher thinks it will be best if we let him make mistakes in his own time.'

'Does he?'

'Yes. So, you don't need to follow him around so closely this time. Watch him, yes. But there's no need for that one-to-one supervision stuff you gave him earlier. Understand?'

'Very well, sir. If that's what you want. Whatever you say. But that's a bit of a change of direction, isn't it?'

'I still want you to keep a dossier. But I don't want Ruff to be under the same pressure you gave him before. It was bad for his health, so Paddy tells me...'

'Right.'

'Well. That's all I can think of right now. Welcome back. I will tell Fart'n Mart'n to hand things over to you. We need him back driving a Panda anyway. I don't need to tell you we're short of manpower.'

'Right sir,' I started to leave.

'*Oh!* And one last thing ... Clarence.'

'Yup?'

'Fart'n Mart'n put *the new girl* on the area car with Ruff.'

'What new girl?'

'Oh, did I not mention her? We have a new Woman Police Constable. Straight out of Hendon. Her first month. She's the first of many more to come. Lots more yet to. So she's been assigned to the area car.'

'Why is that?' I asked. I was surprised they'd put an inexperienced officer on the most critical police resource we had.

'Why is *what*?' asked the Inspector, a touch disgruntled by my direct questioning.

'Why has Fart'n Mart'n put a recruit onto the area car?'

'Because she's the only non-driver right now.'

'What about young Peter Prince?'

'He managed to get a Panda course. Peter is driving Panda Three.'

'Oh. I see.'

52

I left Inspector Beedi to toy with his accordion and went upstairs to find the delightful June Kent. I decided I needed a bit of cheering-up and she'd be the only person in the Nick who might do it. I felt somewhat less-than-encouraged by my 'return to work' with Beedi.

I dragged myself upstairs and arrived at the office door of the Women's Unit. The door was ajar, so I pushed it open — but there was no one around. The place appeared ransacked; the once well-ordered cabinets were left open, precious files littered surfaces, the phone had been disconnected, and posters had been torn from walls. Reports left crumpled on the floor. *What the hell happened?* As I tried to understand what was going on, I heard a tap on the door. I turned to see one of the C.I.D. typists. She stood by the entrance: 'Can I help you?' she asked, in a snooty way, and with a look of barely concealed hostility.

'I'm trying to find Woman Constable June Kent,' I told her.

'Haven't you heard?' she said. 'The Women's Unit has been disbanded. June is over at Quebec Bravo now. All the girls are gone. This is the office of the Detective Chief Inspector. I would respectfully ask you to *piss off*.'

I glanced at her and sighed. I'd only been gone for six weeks, and it seemed like a century.

'Sarge?' said the C.I.D. typist crossed her arms and shrugged. 'Yes, okay, *okay*. I'm going. Thanks for the information.'

53

That morning was the first time I saw our Woman Police Constable fresh out of Hendon. The first time I saw the brand-new, apprentice police-officer who had been assigned to our most significant policing asset — the wireless car.

After my demoralizing visit to the despoiled office of the Women's Special Unit, I sheepishly attended the canteen. I wandered in unnoticed, still pondering what other significant changes had occurred in my absence. It didn't take me long to see that the entire social structure of my relief team had changed beyond recognition...

All eyes were on *her*.

An animated game of knock-out whist had gained momentum and the exciting centrepiece of the game, the Empress, sat on her throne surrounded by devotees and acolytes. She took the position that Ruff formerly occupied — 'head' of the table: the focal point of all eyes. For a few moments, I couldn't even locate Ruff. He'd shrunken in stature and had been demoted to a backseat position. He sat on a plastic chair, pushed behind the girl — a menial *hireling*. He'd been expelled from the main body, though retained in a new role, he acted as her squire.

I watched the game develop. The new girl stuck a playing card onto her forehead just like Ruff once did: 'This one's double wrapped to keep the flavour in,' she announced, even using *his* singalong style of expression. She slapped the playing card on the tabletop and gave a piggish snort. Then studied her admirers, to evaluate whether they smiled enough, approved abundantly, and applauded sufficiently. Of course, the congregation laughed and clapped in unison. The deal seemed to be: if you adored her suitably, she might return a favour. They all wanted a millisecond of the plonk's smile or perhaps a personalized nod. If you were lucky, it seemed, you might gain a nudge on the shoulder or a furtive poke. Yep, in those moments I determined that this Empress was a mantrap.

My God, though, the girl was incredible: A skilled enchantress. She was not pretty-pretty. Not in the conventional sense, not like the models you see on Page 3 of the currant-bun. She was no pin-up — and I mean that in so far as she wasn't merely bosoms and teeth. She was *much more*. Much more! She was the most *complete* woman I had ever seen. She had a sort of mystical beauty — I later described her: *rare and alluring*. She exploited her divine grace, and it sent men crazy. Her statuesque body was noble and well-proportioned. She sat as tall as Ruff, so looked him in the eye. Her face appeared fully spherical, and perhaps her best feature was the broad forehead. Her brow had been given extra emphasis by a brutally secured ponytail that caught her yellow-blond hair, creating a golden cap. This cap of yellow reminded me of the zucchetto worn by a Pope. The undocked tail of her hair hung to her waist like a thick sausage of bright flaxen streams. Twisted and plump, her ponytail resembled gilded rope. And the arched crest above each of her blue-violet eyes was double-edged with dark lashes. With the brows pencilled-in to add extra detail. Each brow line had an edgy, sharp-pointed boundary.

Her lips were full and waxily fruitful — vividly beamish — she shared secret smiles and witty quips with all her adherents in turn. Her mood seemed unquenchable and irresistible. While her perfect, orb-like head appeared to balance on a soaring white neck. The neck was narrow, virtually snake-like — with a super-hypnotic nape. I noticed a hint of dewiness near her earlobes, and I could not draw my eyes away from the area. More than anything, I wanted to go over and pull my nails across the paleness of her throat. I wanted to tap the splendid soft cartilage near her chin and linger on the perfect larynx before I gazed at the skin that led to her breast. How I fixated on her purity...

Then I heard a shout that snapped-me-out of my delight: 'Here comes Sargey...' Ruff stood and pushed his chair back. He lolloped towards me and possessed the bright smile of someone who'd found true contentment. He grabbed my elbow and pulled me towards the canteen table. I read the faces: the Constables seemed pleased to see me. Wally West, Peter Prince, Charlie M.C. Butler and even Fart'n Mart'n. But I understood I hadn't been brought over to be re-acquainted with old chums. No, this was a *formal presentation*. A royal introduction if you like. I was about to be a debutante: and her highness might confer pleasure upon me.

The new girl played her part to perfection. Demurely, she glanced away, until formally beckoned to acknowledge my presence. Ruff pushed his chubby hand into the small of my back and thrust me forward to greet her. As he did so, he announced my presence to her divine majesty, 'May I present our new and brightest relief member. Sergeant? I have great pleasure in introducing you to W.P.C. Elita du Maurier.'

Elita glanced up when she heard her name. She gave me a beautiful smile. She opened her lips wide enough to expose a hint of super-white teeth

'Elita...' continued Ruff. 'This is Sergeant Chesterfield... I told you about him.'

Like any lady of good breeding, she remained seated. But loosely held out long fingers for me to grasp. She said, 'The pleasure is mine, I'm sure. It's good to meet you, finally, Sergeant. I heard so many good things. Please take a seat.'

I shook Elita's hand. Then — horror of horrors — she scrunched her forehead. Those wrinkles were, undoubtedly, a sign that something had gone wrong. *Surely, I hadn't screwed things up already had I?* No, Lady Elita conveyed her sudden displeasure of Ruff's uncouth manners. 'Rufus, you big fat lunk-head, don't make the Sergeant occupy a side-chair...' she scolded. 'Give him *yours*. He will sit *by me*.'

'I'm sorry,' Ruff said as he slid his chair to me and took a spare one from a stack *even further back*. And that's how she altered the hierarchy of our group. Appropriate to my rank, she granted me a position by her side, the *consigliere* of her wishes —the role of second-in-command, conferred with immediate effect. And she bestowed a new responsibility on Ruff too — from now on he would be her muscleman and protector. All others were lackeys. They sat in a circle around her throne and clung to her nuances. Now we would *all* be eager participants in the court of Elita.

54

After knock-out whist, cigarettes and wee-wees, the relief convened in the station yard for a conflab. 'You want to come out with us on the car Sargey?' Elita asked. She didn't bother to consult Ruff. Mindful of what I'd been advised by the Inspector beforehand — i.e. to cut Ruff a slice of slack — I declined her kind offer and instead chose to grab a ride-along with Wally West. Wally is about as ho-hum a policeman as you would ever find: ditchwater dull, harmless, and thoroughly unremarkable. In other words, he'd be the perfect copper to pair up with if you'd just returned to work after a nasty accident and wanted to 'tread carefully'. Nevertheless, it wasn't long before a serious call came over our bat-phones that made even Wally perk up.

It seemed the area car had already screamed to the scene of a severe assault; they received the call via the R/T set via a message sent from Information Rom — and they were on the look-out for a suspect who'd made-off from the scene, on foot. Another Panda had arrived and reported that a male had been brutally assaulted. Apparently, the story emerged that an assailant had shown-up from a nearby railway station and had laid into another guy in broad daylight. The victim was a down-at-heel turf-accountant on his way to a grubby little office, so the best guess was that the attack was to settle an old gambling score. Whatever the motive had been, it was an unmistakable an act of supreme aggression.

Young Peter Prince had arrived at the scene first, and he called-up with a note of urgency in his voice: 'Skipper if you are coming to this you should be warned the injuries are quite significant.'

'Give me an assessment...'

'Well, the guy is out cold. It looks as if he's been shot in the head. Though witnesses deny any firearm has been involved. They say the geezer was hit by a blunt weapon. The victim is in his sixties. He doesn't respond. Ambulance on the way.'

'Out to you. Any unit have an update on the suspect?'

Elita, the new girl, was next to speak: 'Yes, Sarge. Three-o-five here. The suspect is male R.C.1. aged thirty wearing a light beige Harrington jacket. The informant described him as a boot-boy. Probably headed toward Embassy Road.' I thought Elita expressed herself commendably on the radio. She possessed a silver-tongued voice of cockle-shell and plum. Typical English pedigree, I suppose.

In due course, and at his standard tortoise-pace, Wally West drove me the scene of the crime. Once we got there, I saw the L.A.S. had arrived, and the attendant gave an assortment of expressions, all of which looked decidedly grim. The other ambulance crewman worked on the casualty, but I saw by his mien he didn't have high hopes for the man's recovery.

'To all units —' I transmitted, 'This is an ugly attack. Treat the suspect with extreme caution. Don't tackle him without back-up. Quebec Mike did you receive?'

'Received and understood. We will inform the duty officer and C.I.D.'

A shopkeeper came over to provide an account: 'As far as I could make out, the bother-boy hit him once. He used a cudgel. I saw the thing in his hand. He clouted the man real hard, across the head. Down the guy went. The criminal walked away as if nothing happened. That's the funny thing; he didn't even run. He merely sauntered...' The shopkeeper indicated towards a line of shops. Some of the businesses had fallen on hard times and either closed for good or were in the process of shutting; a few, such as the dry-cleaners, the betting shop, and the newsagents — from where this witness emerged— clung to customers. 'He went off that way...' he suggested.

'Did you see what he was wearing?'

'Light brown jacket. Brown trousers. No, not really.'

'Did he carry anything with him? What was in his hand?'

'A tool perhaps?'

'What was this tool? Perhaps a knife, maybe?'

'No. Something big and heavy. To strike a blow. Like I told them on the phone, a cudgel, maybe.'

Our units scooted around the area. But it seemed that the suspect was well gone. He'd possibly managed to double back and enter the station to get himself on the next train.

'Perhaps, one day, we will have cameras set up everywhere. Can you imagine that?' I remarked to the witness. 'Things like this will be filmed. We'd see where the suspect went...'

'What? Like in Orwell's Nineteen Eighty-Four? Surveillance on every street corner? I don't think so,' said the man. Judging by the look on his face, the witness was not in favour of *that* idea.

'But cameras would catch baddies, wouldn't they?' I said, trying to persuade him.

'I suppose.'

Then the area car returned. The blue Rover purred along the road edge and pulled to a halt. Elita emerged as the ambulance crew began to take away the victim on a stretcher.

'One moment, love. I will be with you in a blink of an eye,' I said. I needed to attract the attention of Constable West first. 'Wally... will you do me a favour?' I shouted. 'Go with the victim to the hospital. Go in the ambulance. For continuity. Make a few notes in your pocketbook along the way. Stay with him when you get there. I will come and collect you when I finish.'

'Aye aye, Skipper.'

I turned to the new female Constable: 'I'm sorry about that love. What were you saying?'

Elita stood graceful and patient by my side. A willowy deity in a world of ugliness. I could make out a faded smell of expensive perfume that originated near her cleavage. The fragrance made me feel light-headed. Her blond ponytail sparkled in the weak sun, and her marvellous smile added a touch of class — perhaps even joy — to a positively forbidding scene. 'I was about to volunteer myself.' she said. 'I want to try to find the weapon —'

'Oh? Okay.'

'I told Ruff that it's likely he got rid of it. Quickly too. He couldn't risk being stopped with the weapon.'

'You think it's possible? I mean, to find it?'

'Why not? I will work forwards from the crime scene. I'll check waste-bins and drains along the way. He can't have taken it far...'

'Well, I imagine it would be a good thing if we could locate it.' I moved my head closer — audaciously closer actually — then I invited her to bend an ear. She did so with a smile, 'It looks bad...' I whispered. 'Treat this as a serious. Profoundly serious.'

'I already told Ruff that this should be treated as *attempted murder.' Have you now?* I was surprised by her precocity. Although I nodded agreement.

So Elita moved away to search for the weapon.

I watched her drift off towards the empty shops and thought she possessed the type of poise and cool-headed self-assurance that could only come from urbane breeding and an excellent education.

Ruff stepped over to me and lit himself a B&H. 'Wonderful, isn't she?' Clearly, he approved of the way she carried herself on those elongated legs.

'Good god, yes,' I replied. I couldn't take my eyes from her elegant form.

'She makes the others look like halfwits,' he mumbled.

'Take care of her Ruff—' I told him, 'She might be full of confidence. But she's made of skin and bones. When she's cut, she bleeds. When she's sad, she cries. Your job is to protect her.'

Ruff nodded and inhaled: 'Look at her now,' he said. 'She reckons she can find the weapon. It's the best chance we have of nabbing the nasty shit who's responsible for this vile attack.'

And as Ruff uttered these words, we heard Elita call-up over her bat-phone. She was just out of sight, her view obscured by a red telephone box: 'Four-one-three? Want to come over? I have located the weapon. '

'Amazing,' said Ruff. 'How long was that? A minute and a half?'

'It's a hammer' she continued. 'Quebec Mike create a station message for me. Time of origin right now. Weapon located by me. At number 112a.' I went with Ruff along the road, and we saw Elita crouched by a doorway at one of the empty shops. The glass entrance had an opening at the bottom, a flapless letter slot, about six inches from the ground. 'He stuffed it in here...' announced Elita. 'About twenty yards from the crime scene.'

'How did you know?' I asked.

'Well, I realized he must have concealed it nearby. I imagined it would be hidden where it wouldn't be found for days. Luck really...'

'Can you see it?' I said, as I peered through the fogged glass of the door and was sure I saw absolutely *nothing*. But then I determined the shaft of a hammer. It rested on top of a layer of crumpled mail.

'See how it rests on the old letters?' she explained, 'We can assume it's been freshly put there. We will get some idea of the date by looking at the most recent postmark of the top letter.'

'I wonder if we have key-holder details for this shop? Seems, unlikely if the store has gone out of business...'

I was about to get on the radio and ask Quebec Mike if they could assist with key-holder details when Elita bent down on all fours. 'I think I can get it...' she said. 'Hold on...'

She undid her right cuff then pushed her sleeve to expose a slender arm adorned with light-golden tufts. She extended her fabulously groomed fingers and entered them into the slot. To extend her reach further, she had to move her body around so that her bottom was on the floor and her legs akimbo. She stared into my face while she did this and gave a concentrated grimace. All this while she flexed her over-stretched fingers into the hole, in an attempt to grip the hammer. I watched her expression. Her grimace transformed from endeavour to pleasure. Bit by bit, she had managed to ease the hammer out. She delicately held the part of the tool that's located between the handle and the head. She held the thick oily shaft with slender fingers. It was a fantastic feat of dexterity. *She's done that sort of thing before,* I pondered.

'Good gravy. It's a heavy bugger—' she declared. She wriggled her arm free and moved from her contorted position. She placed the tool onto the pavement. 'It's a claw hammer.'

Ruff and I peered at the mean-looking instrument. That thing could do a lot of damage. One swipe would kill a man.

'Ruff, dearest... Do you mind going to the newsagent for me, my love? Grab a large envelope? So, we can put the hammer away safely. The envelope will have to be brand new, honey, so you might have to pay for it.' Ruff received his instructions, so marched off gallantly to do the lady's bidding.

'We need to get this properly bagged-up,' she explained. 'So that's why I need a clean envelope.'

'Of course,' I mumbled.

Then Elita turned over once more, this time to reveal more of her opaque black tights than perhaps she'd wanted. I glimpsed the cotton gusset and even a tantalizing flash of white panties. '*Oooh!* Did I give you a flash of my knickknacks there Sargey? Sorry—' she chuckled as she rolled her tummy along the floor. 'It's just that I wanted to grab the top letter too. So, we can establish the date on the postmark and keep it as an exhibit. Good idea, eh?'

I grunted 'Yeah' but to be honest, this young lady was thinking too fast for me to keep up. I would never — in a month of Sundays — have thought of doing *all this*. So Elita managed to get hold of the topmost window envelope. She dragged it out of the flap and showed it to me. It was a bill reminder, and the envelope was date-stamped two days previous. Ruff returned with a sturdy Manila bag, so he plopped the hammer inside.

'There will be fingerprints on the shaft, no doubt—' said Elita. 'And there is no way the shit-head got it down there into that slot without leaning on the tiles.' She indicated the door 'step', and I noticed it was the same level as the footway but tiled to make it stand-out. 'Can you call the S.O.C.O?' she added.

Before I called Quebec Mike to initiate a visit from the Scenes of Crimes officer, I was called by Constable Wally West. 'Sarge just to inform you. The doctor here at A&E is saying we should treat this as manslaughter. He hasn't pronounced life extinct yet, but he wanted you to know it is going to be the likely outcome...'

'Received Wally. Please stay with the victim, and we will start working this end to get hold of next of kin. Quebec Mike, did you receive that update from Constable West?'

'Yes. Thanks. I've been monitoring. Our C.I.D. is on the way. For your information.'

'Noted. And, to inform you that we have preserved the weapon that was used in the crime. Please inform the S.O.C.O. And ask him to attend our present location...' And at that point, I had to stop, because I was not sure why the S.O.C.O. was required to participate. I looked to Elita for inspiration.

'The S.O.C.O. needs to dust the tiles under the mail slot...' she explained. 'The assailant must have touched those when he bent to deposit the hammer. Besides, the S.O.C.O. needs to take possession of the hammer. That's essential if we want to preserve the evidentiary chain...'

'Oh, I see,' I said.

the Franz Klammer

The Sorry and the Sad

We all knew it would take several days for the fingerprint boys at C.O. to manually process the dabs removed from the weapon that Elita had found hidden in the shop doorway. The C.I.D. had a hunch that they knew the identity of the criminal behind the hammer-attack. A murder squad was formed, and a raid organized. The next morning we'd be doing 'a spot of carpentry' as the detective sergeant told us the previous evening, 'That's to say,' he explained, 'We'll be putting a few doors in.'

———

I planned to meet Ruff and Elita early for a nice cup of Rosy Lee in the canteen. I arrived by four a.m. and, because I was first to arrive, I filled the night-duty tea kettle and started to make a pot of tea. Night shift were still on the ground, doing final checks so the place was nice and quiet. The first of our team to arrive was Elita. Even at the crack of dawn she looked sensational: 'Hiya Sargey. How are you doing?'

'Good, particularly good. Nice to see you, you're bright early.'

'Oh? I get up around *now*. To muck out horses and clean the stables.'

'You have horses?'

'Yes, two. Freddie and Ginger.'

'Do you live with your parents?'

'Well, until I went to Hendon I did, yes. But now I rent a ground floor flat a mile or two along the road. It's situated halfway between my parents pile and my yard.'

'You own a yard?'

'No, silly. It's a livery yard that I part-share. It's where Freddie and Ginger are stabled.'

'So, you muck out every day? Like every day at four o'clock?'

'Well, I'm lucky. I part-own my boys with one of our grooms, she shares duties... I only have to be up at the crack of dawn four maybe five times a week...'

'Forgive me asking, but how do you afford to run horses and rent an apartment on forty quid a week?'

'My dad is generous. He provides a monthly allowance.'

'Wow. That *is* generous.' I paused before I asked the next question because I wanted to get the 'sense of the words' right. 'Sorry to intrude like this. But why did you join the police? I just can't think why! Surely your parents don't approve?'

'They're fine with it. They have always let me do what I wanted to do. And it's no secret I wanted to do this job since I was young...'

'I imagine you will want to go into Mounted Division?'

'*God, no.* Their work involves constant grooming. Followed by a shitty football match dealing with hooligans, or maybe a guard-change. For me riding is a hobby —a diversion — I would *hate* to do it as my job...'

'Oh?'

'Actually, I would like to be a detective. My father says I ought to aim high. I want to be Detective Superintendent by thirty.'

'How old are you now — if you don't mind me asking?'

'Twenty-three.'

'Christ!' I was surprised to hear that. I'd already calculated she must be around twenty-eight. She had the composure and confidence of a mature adult.

'Do you want me to do that?' She saw I'd been holding the kettle under the cold tap for ages.

'Sorry.' I put my mind back to the job. I filled the kettle and spooned half a packet of dry leaves into the enamel pot. 'Do you have a boyfriend or fiancé?'

'*Ha ha!* No. Why do they always ask that?' She gave a canny glance. 'I knew lots of lovely fellas when I was at school. I lost contact with them when I went to College. I met some nice guys there, too. Unfortunately, I lost touch with *everyone* once I went to Hendon.'

'You went to university?' A university education is almost unheard-of in the Police. Even the deputy commissioner didn't have letters after his name. Unless you counted the Q.P.M.

'Yes. Like me, many girls I met at Hendon I did higher education *first* before embarking a career in the police service.'

'What do you think of Ruff?' I ventured, radically changing the subject.

'Ruff? He's sweet.'

'He's married, you know...'

'Gosh, yes, of course, I know. I've met the lovely Mrs. Palmerston. Eve is her name. She's adorable. Why? Why did you feel the need to remind me that he was married?'

'He is *umm...*' I wanted to say something along the lines of: 'Because Ruff wants to get inside your bloomers and bang you senseless.' But I had the feeling such a line wouldn't go down too well with a bird who'd been to university, rented her own flat and rode horses for relaxation. Plus, I didn't know that it was *true* (about Ruff fancying her, I mean). So, I tiptoed around the issue: 'Ruff really *likes* you,' I explained, careful not to tip into anything more contentious. 'I think he's developed, um, feelings...' she gazed into my eyes when I paused. 'I mean, he's developed feelings *for you* —'

Elita was about to reply when we heard the approaching *brmm!* as

Ruff's knackered jalopy bumbled into the station yard. Moments later, the canteen doors swung open and in stepped the big fellah himself. The Met's manliest copper: 'Sorry I'm late treacle. Tea on?' He planted a kiss on Elita's cheek. Elita smiled in my direction and gave a discreet wink. I guessed the smirk she also gave was a temporary reprieve. Though I also foresaw that things were about to get a whole lot more uncomfortable around this pair.

Soon our other playmates arrived. The detectives looked particularly disheveled. They were not used to getting up so early. Mostly C.I.D. were nine-to-five wallers. They carried with them an assortment of cricket items: wicket keeping pads, white gloves, and cricket boxes. One even brought a load of bats.

'Are we going to play cricket?' Elita asked. She delivered this serious question with a charming smile.

'No miss. We're doing a job of carpentry,' replied the bleary-eyed Detective Sergeant who oversaw the briefing and the raid. All the blokes chuckled. 'Right, let's get a cup of Rosy down us —' he announced, 'Then we'll get kitted up.' The officers had already begun to thrust cricket boxes down their pants and strap pads to their shins.

'Opening time is anytime!' Ruff cried out, in his sing-song voice. We joined him with a clap of hands.

55

When we arrived at Myrtle Grove to execute our warrant, the C.I.D parked their cars out of sight. Ruff hid the 'obo' van we'd arrived in behind a row of trees. The murder squad detectives had already given us —mere 'wooden tops' — the less glamorous task of going round the back of the premises to seal-off any escape route used by the suspect. The C.I.D lads wanted the glory of 'going in' through the front door to make the arrest.

The plain-clothes mob waited for us to sneak around the back of the building; they hesitated for two minutes before they stepped off, so we could adequately set ourselves up.

When Elita, Ruff and I slipped around the back of 33 Myrtle Grove, we trod warily. We were careful not to overturn dustbins or alert neighbourhood dogs. A back-yard tomcat gave a surprised hiss and arched its back at us before it decided we were no threat and walked off in a huff. And Ruff did his best to blend in against a wall, with his red hair matching the pink brickwork. Meanwhile, Elita and I hid near a coal bunker. We dipped down low so we could not be seen from any of the upstairs rooms.

56

I studied the building while Elita and I huddled close in the morning darkness. The premises seemed to comprise of five self-contained flatlets. All entry was via the front door — where the C.I.D were headed. Only the ground floor apartment had a rear entrance. So that's where *we* needed to focus our attention. 'This is the best place to be —' I whispered to Elita. 'If he escapes through the back door, we'll have him.'

I presumed that she nodded in agreement because I was clobbered by a braid of her long, blonde, ponytailed hair as it swung across my face to thump me in the eyes. Elita stifled a giggle: 'I am sorry, Sargey —' she murmured. 'I was checking-on Ruff's hideout. He seems *very* well hidden.'

From the wonderful closeness of our confined position — knelt on the damp ground — I distinguished Elita's soft heartbeat and even sensed her mint-scented breath against the side of my cheek. I savoured such a heavenly moment. Then I heard three dongs on the bat-phone. Three *dongs* were the traditional signal — made by flicking the talking brooch on the radio — to indicate that the 'entry team' would be 'going in.' From our location in the backyard, we felt the reverberating sounds of boots crushing against timber and shoulders heaving against metal hinges — as limbs got slammed against cold oak. There was no splintering crunch sound, though. So, I assumed the 'boot and shoulder' tactic had *not* been effective. The door didn't *go in*.

Speediness is essential in these circumstances, so when we heard the tinkling of glass, we realized the C.I.D had changed tactics and instead smashed their way through using the front windows. The murder squad were now entering the property via the front bays.

So much for carpentry, I thought. *The filth were practising glaziery.*

Not long after the sounds of breaking glass — *all hell broke loose.* We heard shouts, screams and a dog barking wildly. Next, we heard pots and pans being thrown around ostentatiously. There were further dings, clangs, and yells as it sounded like a troupe of amateur dramatists were enacting a parody of a sizeable disturbance. I'd never heard such a commotion in my life.

Then we heard a distinctive noise.

Three blasts from a shrill whistle. *Yup!* We heard it again.

Three sharp peeps.

The peeps were made by an instrument that was *awfully familiar* to us. The peeps came from a British Bobby's standard-issue silver whistle. Famous the world-over — each London Copper has been 'armed' with this vital piece of equipment since the nineteenth century. Three urgent whistle-blows meant only one thing: An officer was in trouble; he required immediate assistance. It seemed as if the raid on the house was going to rat-shit.

'Are we going?' Elita asked.

'Not on your nelly...' I told her. The very last thing we should do was move from our position near the back door. We had to hold our nerve.

Then we saw Ruff move away from the wall. 'Where's he going?' Elita whispered. Ruff teetered by the side as he heard the whistle sounds. Then it looked like he decided to move on. *Oh shit! He's going to help the filth,* I thought. *He'd been lured by the whistle blasts!*

Elita saw what was developing — so she cried out in vain, 'Ruff. Don't leave us. Don't you see? It's a deception. They are trying to create a diversion!' But we watched Ruff trudge off.

His huge lolloping strides made gigantic crunching noises on the gravel by the side of the building. Once he'd gone out of sight, I felt my heart rate increasing. My vision became clearer, and my sense of hearing grew acute. I distinguished that *something* was happening. I felt the hairs on the back of my neck prickle with static electricity.

Then the warm breath from Elita became deeper. I felt her hand grab my arm.

We saw it together.

At first, I perceived a vague shape. A brown-red silhouette made of something gaseous. Then this nebulous form became substance, and we both realized, at the same time, the form was a man. I heard Elita gasp as she squeezed my arm.

A shadow-man crawled out of the uppermost story of the house we were watching. He gently slipped-open a casement window then dropped his toes onto an ornamental balustrade situated beneath his feet. He allowed the stone ridge to take his weight. *He'd tried this before*, I thought. The figure crouched low and allowed his long legs to dangle. Then he let his limbs swing, bit-by-bit, and lowered himself to the next level. Once he had dropped down, he edged along to a drainpipe and shinned down that till he reached the ground.

I immediately sprang into action. I jumped from my hiding place by the coal bunker and rushed him. I hoped the man was dead-tired after his long climb.

He was not.

At the very instant, it really mattered — when I was a mere twelve inches from the man — he evaded me. With a subtle twist of his body, he reacted. He punched me solidly and powerfully in the solar plexus. Where it did me the most harm. I went down like a sack of spuds. Disabled. Winded.

I heard a giant commotion from behind and saw Elita dash for it. I grasped what she was about to do, even though I rolled on the floor: she was going to tackle the figure. I attempted to holler *No!* but, as I tried to yell, the agony hurtled through my bones and nearly made me pass out. My back was still tender from the accident, of course, and my kidneys felt as if they were bursting from my body.

Elita moved fast. Like a panther on steroids. The male was only able to run a few steps when I saw her pull him down. She tackled the bloke as if she was a rugby-league professional. But he squirmed and wriggled like a mad man. Soon enough, he had the better of her. His pure animal strength was too much for her. And as I watched helplessly, I saw him wrench his legs free of her grasp then snake his thighs around her blonde skull to smash her head against the cruel concrete. I saw him half-stand, and so I tried to shout 'No' again.

It was then that Elita experienced the *magic moment* — the instant when a bad 'un realizes he's about to thump a Bobby in full uniform — it's a fatal and momentary lack of focus caused by what we Copper's term the *Colgate Ring of Confidence*— triggered by our blue garb. The pause was to be the man's comeuppance.

Because — at that moment — I saw *another* large figure spring from nowhere. It was a mass of furiously bounding, fuming audacity. It was Ruff.

I saw Ruff's fist collide with the suspect's face. It knocked a tooth free. The first blow was followed by several more pitiless shots aimed at the upper body of the suspect. The man went down. And this time, for good.

Ruff to the rescue: 'You didn't think I'd let you down, did you?' he yelled. He reclined on the suspect's backbone and pulled the brooch of his bat-phone to the side of his mouth. 'Quebec Mike. One in custody. In the back garden. Can I get some help on the hurry-up? Plus, a set of handcuffs. Call an ambulance too. The skipper is down. I repeat. The skipper is down.'

57

Once the prisoner had been handcuffed and taken to Quebec Mike, I got myself checked over by the ambulance crew. Ruff joined me at the front of the house. He'd lit a new B&H and sat his fat arse on the step: 'Elita has taken the body...' he told me, as he lit up. 'One for murder. Not a bad arrest for a probationer, eh? She deserves it, doesn't she?'

'Not bad at all mate.'

'How do you feel?'

'I feel shocking. I told the ambulance guys I was fine, but my kidneys are cattle-trucked, and my back is sore as a whore on a Saturday night...'

'Why not take a couple of days sick?'

'*Nah*! I'll be right as rain after a cup of Rosy Lee.'

'Alrighty. You want a stiffener before I give you a lift to the nick?' Ruff produced a hipflask and twisted off the cap.

'Not in public Ruff. For the love of fuck ...'

He took a sip of liquor then wiped the top. 'Are you sure?' I sniffed the whiskey but pushed it away.

'Right. Let's get you back to the station Sargey,' he said.

We wandered to the 'observation van', and both jumped in. Ruff found the keys under the sun-visor. 'I saw him at the window, you know...' he whispered.

'Who?'

'I saw the fellow who punched you, you know, the main suspect. He pulled back his curtains to get a better look. I suppose he was assessing his backyard to see if he could work out where the police would be hidden. The geezer has lots of form, so he *knew* we'd be round the back *too*, he isn't stupid. I'm sure he saw me. But I'm confident he didn't glimpse you or Elita because you had a better hiding place. He'd noticed me when I took my song-and-dance to get the fuck out of there, giving *him* the impression I was going around the front to investigate the clamour. That's when he thought it was all clear to climb out the window.'

'So, you *never* left your post?'

'No, of course I bloody didn't. That would have been a basic mistake.'

58

The day after I'd been clobbered by the 'contract killer' in Myrtle Grove, I was back on my feet and raring to go again.

I was not actually as fit as a fiddle, though: my nerves tingled, and my stomach felt pained, but I reckoned I could probably manage another shift, so I hitched a lift with Charlie 'M.C.' Butler on Panda Three. In the past, I hadn't seen eye-to-eye with Constable Butler. To be frank, I'd found him outspoken, intolerant and, honestly, a bigot. I hoped we might draw a line under our past disagreements.

'Of course, she has not lifted a finger for herself — never once,' Charlie M.C. Butler announced as soon as we rumbled out of the Nick and down Park Drive.

'Who? Who are you moaning about? Is it Elita?' I asked.

'It's always the same with these fancy bints. They merely wait to be licked and rammed. By the unsuspecting idiots who buzz around the gash like blue-bottles attracted to turds.'

'Erm? Well, I think she attended college and graduated. She did *that* for herself. And from what I saw the other day — Elita is not afraid to get stuck in. She even mucks out horses...'

'Mucks out horses, *ha*...' Charlie Butler gave a derisive snort. 'She lures the guys with fanny juice, doesn't she? All she need do is smile, and they'll come running like they're ponies on heat. I'm not saying she's a whore — I am just saying she's a daddy's girl — a fucking user.' He glared into my eyes as he said the next bit: 'Beware, Sergeant. She'll get her claws into you *next*. The bitch knows what she's up to. She knows how to draggle a man by his prick. She'll play you like a puppet... a puppet that hangs from one of her dangling pubes. If you know what I mean.'

'Actually, I don't *know what you mean*. I think you may have got her all wrong —' The last thing I needed was a lecture from Charlie M.C. Butler.

But he hadn't finished with the sermon: 'Really? Why did she come into the Job then? Why?'

'Honestly, I don't know. I haven't a clue — '

'I'll tell you *why* shall I...' He took a breath. 'She came into this Job for a laugh. To share hilarious yarns with upper-class friends. To have a few jokes at us common folk's expense. She'll tell them, for example, how she fucked a working man.'

'Who did she fuck?'

'It's obvious, isn't it?' M.C. replied. 'And they'll all hoot about it down the polo club, won't they? Around a tray of cocktails.' Constable Butler pulled the Panda into a tight parking space just yards from the Nick, to fetch his morning paper and twenty ciggies.

'No, it is not —' I shouted. 'Who's she shagging?'

'Ruff. The poor old twerp. Clings to her every word, doesn't he? He's enraptured, besotted, and obsessed by the snobbish witch. He's like a pathetic puppy-dog when *she's* about.'

'*Nah!* Ruff would never shag out of wedlock. He loves his old lady...' I argued. 'He might be tempted by a younger girl, but would never shag around...'

'Well, he's not lived up to my expectations, that's all I am saying. I thought that he would be the man who'd slap-her-down. Keep the little madam docile. But no, he's allowed her to queen-bitch it over us. Over all of us. She needs a good hard smack, that's my opinion, and I genuinely thought Ruff was the right man for the job. But I misjudged him. He isn't *brave enough* to raise a finger to her. He won't clobber her like she deserves. He's turned into a fucking mouse. The posh bint has him eating out of her middle-class fingers.'

M.C. Butler slammed the Panda and strutted off to the newspaper shop.

'What a fuck-twat,' I said softly.

59

I could not stand another minute with the narrow-minded git M.C. Butler — so I swapped things around right after refreshments and took a ride out with young P.C. Prince instead.

'What do you think of Elita?' I asked.

'Cocky bint isn't she? Presumptuous. Don't know what else to say.'

'Is she? Cocky, I mean?'

'Yes, I would say-so. Don't forget she's only got three months in the Job yet she's already operating on the wireless car. She even told Paddy Gallaher she wanted to go on the next Advanced Car course when it came up. She requested a Panda course on the day she arrived. It took me over a year to get *that*. Ruff says he's a hundred per cent behind her getting the next Advanced Course. What's wrong with him? Doesn't he know that I've got more service than *her*...'

'Don't you think she's earned it though?'

'No, of course *not*. Don't get me wrong; she's had a lot of good bodies. She's had more crime arrests in two months than I've had in my entire service... but that doesn't mean anything...'

'Doesn't it?'

'She's even nicked someone for murder, for fuck's sake. But the experience must be earned, mustn't it, Sarge? Probationers must do their time on the shop floor before they get advancement. They have to make tea, empty the bins, wipe-up the puke, feed the stray dogs, help in the property store and do all the odd jobs. I'm not seeing Elita doing any of the kind of shit I spent a year doing... During my first year, I was gaoler, assistant station officer, comms officer, school crossing patrol and every other numpty fucking job they could think of to keep me off the streets. I wasn't swanning around in a wireless car from *day one* like some kind of fairytale Princess. If I were, maybe I'd have had crime arrests too. They've allowed Elita to act like she owns the fucking place. She gets everything she wants, and she gets it *right now*. She's not willing to bide her time, and I don't think it's right. But that's just my opinion.'

'Don't you think that's an old way of thinking? Don't you think probationers these days — especially ones of her calibre — should be treated differently?'

'Maybe, I don't know. It doesn't feel right. Maybe, I suppose.'

'How do you get on with her? *Yourself*. I mean?'

'She doesn't say much to me. She looks down her nose if I'm honest. As if I'm immature. I expect she thinks the young ones on this relief are dumb wits. She prefers the older guys. She likes you and Ruff.'

'She likes me?'

'Course she does Sarge! She thinks you're a diamond...'

'May I ask a sensitive question?'

'Go on — '

'Do you think she's banging Ruff?'

'Well, I would not be surprised if she *was*,' said the young Constable. 'They are close, aren't they? They spend a lot of time together. People say she likes his unsophisticated ways. You know — she wants to taste some rough. She wants to get her claws into a geezer what's born on the wrong side of the tracks, so to speak...'

'But Ruff is happily married. He wouldn't stray, would he?'

'He's *bewizzled* by her...'

I looked at Peter Prince and gave a perplexed stare: 'I do not know that word. I never heard it before. What does it mean?'

'It's a combination: it means befuddled, bewildered and bewitched. Ruff is a muddle-headed fool. He's flattered by the attention she's giving. He's bewizzled.'

'I see.'

60

Shortly after 1:30 p.m., the big call came in.

Information Room at M.P. boomed-in with authority over our personal radio system: 'Quebec Mike, Quebec Mike. Central station hold up alarm. Vere and Glyn Bank, 12 Embassy Road. Raid in progress. Repeat, raid in progress. All Quebec Mike units to respond...'

Pandas 1 to 3 responded. There was no van available: thanks to the shoddy management of the duties by Fart'n Mart'n while I was away. The idiot had allowed both van drivers — Godfrey Lambert and Dave Yale — to be on leave at the same time. So M.P. got all the resources we had at our disposal. Peter Prince and I accepted the call, and we started to make our way to the bank. We made good progress by the judicious flashing of our headlamps and the beeping of the Panda horn.

Ruff and Elita were posted to the wireless car. Elita had already announced they would go to one of the main traffic junctions on our ground —not directly to the scene — to sit and wait for the getaway car. This common-sense preparation paid off immediately. We heard Elita's honeyed tones just a few moments after the call came out, on the personal radio. She transmitted in a composed and unflustered manner: 'Just to advise you Quebec Mike. We are currently in pursuit of a suspect vehicle. Three up. A gold Granada that's heading towards Stanmore. We are conducting a commentary on the main set. Out to you.'

'Wow...' Peter said, 'They've got themselves a chase.' Information Room patched-through the 'chase' so we could listen-in.

'Left, left, left into Ashford drive. Speed 50....'

'Good. Keep it going' said the man in the Information Room.

'Now left again. Into Bristol Avenue...'

'Left into Bristol Avenue. Received.'

'Now right, right, right into Country Way.'

'Noted.'

'The vehicle is slowing down in Country Way. We just passed by Everest House. Hold on...'

We waited, with high expectations. The Elita shouted something: 'Yes. One male bailed out— I repeat, one male decamped. Made off on foot carrying a bag. Heading towards the garages at the rear of Everest House.'

After that, there was silence.

'Any unit can make their way to Everest House?' asked the guy at Information Room. 'Any dog van respond?' There was a hush. 'Can *anyone* divert to the last location given? We believe it was Everest House?'

We heard Wally West call up on the bat-phone. 'I can go there instead of the bank...' he offered.

'Roger that. Make your way,' suggested Information Room.

There was silence again. For excruciating seconds, we heard nothing. Then the voice of Ruff: 'Right, right, right into Hollywood Drive. I'm still in pursuit...'

Did he say *I'm still in pursuit*? What was Ruff doing on the radio? Elita was the operator. Ruff was the driver. Ruff should have been concentrating on doing his driving, for heaven's sake, not making a radio commentary.

'Received. Do you know what happened at Everest House? The last message received by M.P. was that the male decamped on foot...' said Information room.

'That's correct, M.P. The male is being chased *on foot* by the R/T operator from this unit. She needs help. The bandit car, with the remaining suspects, is still being pursued by me. But I am single manning. Now left, left, left into Main Road. Two suspects on board. Speed fifty.'

'Keep the commentary going. In addition — units now on the hurry-up to the last known position of the R/T operator — believed it's the garages near Everest House.'

'Let's go there,' cried Peter. He made a dramatic handbrake turn, and we headed along a dirt track that would take us quicker to Country Way.

We were a few seconds away from Everest House when we heard Ruff call again on the radio. 'M.P. M.P. and all units. The bandit car has crashed outside the May Pole public house. Tipper Street. Two suspects decamped. I'm now chasing on foot.'

'Good God,' I said. 'This is crazy...' But I admit my adrenaline was pumping like mad through my body. Our Panda car screamed into Country Way. We saw a group of shoppers standing near Everest House. As we approached, we could see other people waving at us frantically. A lady with a stroller pointed towards a thin alley. I jumped out of our Panda even though the wheels were still moving. I shouldn't have done it and felt a twinge to my back, but I ignored it. I ran around a corner, and I saw Elita. She was on the ground.

Her powerful thighs were locked tight around the torso of a male suspect. A bag was nearby, and it bulged with stolen banknotes. 'I have the son of a bitch,' Elita shouted. '*Shhh* —' she said to the man, as he gurgled. 'Sarge. He was armed. There's a sawn-off by his legs. I can't get at it at the moment because he's struggling too much. I cannot move. Would you be a treasure and grab it for me?'

I saw a brown buttstock in the dirt. The gun was resting near the legs of the suspect. I pulled out my handkerchief and quickly wrapped it around the stock, then I grabbed hold of the weapon. The man tried to kick at me, but Elita improved her stranglehold on his throat. I saw his face turn blue.

'We need handcuffs ...' I said to no one in particular.

'He's not going anywhere. Are you my love?' Elita commented. She had full control over the robber. 'Horse riding thighs, you see...'

she giggled. 'I can squeeze the breath out of him all day with these two beauties...'

In all the excitement I forgot about Ruff. Then I heard his voice squeaking out over the radio. 'One male detained M.P. May Pole Public House. Tipper Street. Another male is still outstanding. Believed towards Winston Way. Van on the hurry-up to my location, please. Plus, units to Winston Way to search for the outstanding suspect. Last seen towards Winston Way. RC1 male with a grey jacket, light brown hair. Aged thirty.'

M.P. started to organize units from adjacent neighbourhoods to participate.

I heard a *woof* and saw the Divisional dog van — Quebec Zero — arrive. The smiling dog handler jumped out, and I saw that he clasped a pair of handcuffs with his beefy fingers.

'These might come in handy,' he grinned.

Ruff and Elita worked late into the night with their arrests for armed robbery. And although the third robber fled, the Sweeney Todd had a good idea of his identity. So, once they'd put their cricket clobber on — the night duty C.I.D. plus a few hand-selected members of the robbery team — and Ruff & Elita went around the felon's house to 'put the doors in'

Once all the final suspect was safely in police custody, Ruff and Elita were allowed to go home. It was the end of a very protracted, very demanding — but of course, extraordinarily successful — shift.

61

The next afternoon I went to see Inspector Beedi to seek his permission to write-up the two praiseworthy officers for a commendation. I found Beedi in his office. His piano accordion was safely tucked in its case, and he worked on a stack of paperwork. 'What can I do for you?' he grumbled, as I knocked my knuckles against his open door.

'Should I come back later?' I said. 'Is this a difficult time?'

'No, no. I need a word with you anyway...'

'It's about the robbery arrests yesterday...' I said, with a tentative cough. 'Good arrests by Elita and Ruff, huh?' I suggested.

'The Flying Squad seem impressed,' Beedi replied. 'The blaggers went to court this morning and were remanded in custody. They had form as long as your arm ...'

'And the cash — it was secured by Ruff and Elita. And the firearm seized,' I offered.

'Yep.'

'So, it's a good little job? Heh?'

'The C.I.D. seem to think it went hunky-dory...'

'And you guv'nor? What do you think?' If he had any doubts, I wanted him to express them now before I suggested the commendation.

'I think Ruff was out-of-order...' he mumbled.

Did I hear him right? 'Out of order?'

'Yes. I'm sure he failed to comply with written instructions. I have raked through all the old police orders and directives, but I cannot find a single written memo relating to what he did wrong.' *So that's what the pile of papers on his desk related to.*

'What do you think did he do wrong?' I asked.

'He shouldn't have continued with the car chase once he'd dropped off the young plonk. He shouldn't have left her to fend for herself — she was at the mercy of an armed criminal for God's sake. Imagine the headlines tomorrow if she'd been shot? The Sun's headline would have been: 'Girl Left to Die by Ham-fisted Cops.' It would be the end of my pension. Yours too. And why? Because Ruff went for glory. Like he always does. He always goes for glory but doesn't consider the risks. On this occasion, he continued the chase — single-manning the area car. Have you ever heard of such a thing?'

'No sir, actually I haven't.'

'That must be against the rules, mustn't it? But I'm damned if I can find what rules the bastard broke... That's why I'm hunting through this stack of old memos. But when I find the regulation, I want him stuck on...'

'So, you think his actions put Elita at risk?'

'Well, of course I do. He ought to have stayed with her. He should have waited by her side to help secure the first prisoner. Not dashed off to get the others. Ruff is a loose cannon. His impulsive behaviour will get innocent people killed one of these days. Unless we put a stop to it.'

'I see.'

'But for now, I can't find any instruction that says he has to call a chase off when he drops off the radio operator...' Beedi put his hands behind his head and gazed at me. 'Besides, we have much more disquieting issues to contend with.'

'We do What's that?'

'Yes. Close the door. Take a seat. This is a sensitive issue.'

I clicked the door closed and pulled up one of his metal-framed chairs. I was all-ears.

Inspector Beedi leaned closer and employed lower tones than

usual: 'A night duty Constable — I don't want to reveal the officer's identity at this stage — he heard Ruff and Elita discuss the possibility of an overnight stay at a hotel. A hotel of disrepute. It seems, from the informant, Ruff suggested they should get a drink to 'celebrate' their arrest. When Elita asked where they might get hold of a celebration drink so late at night, Ruff suggested the 'Style Hotel.' Their conversation was overheard.'

'What? The crummy dump in Main Road? The one built on a landfill site? They arranged to go for a drink there?'

'According to the informant, when Ruff suggested the 'Style Hotel' Elita seemed 'happy' at the prospect. It seems probable they spent the night together.'

'*No.*' I shook my head vigorously. 'I don't believe it, sir. For one thing, Elita would never stay in a shithole like 'The Style.' She's got high standards. And Ruff loves his old lady. He wouldn't go over the side.'

'Well, that's the suggestion, anyway. The night duty Inspector has written it all up. He put-it-on-paper for the attention of Superintendent Peter Nikki.'

'Perhaps they popped-in for a swift drinkie before they went home. I might believe that. But I'm sure they didn't stay over. Not together.' I advocated.

'I would agree with you. By and large. And, just like you, I don't like finger-pointing...' Inspector Beedi took a deep breath while I gave him a puzzled frown. 'But other evidence has emerged that supports the original accusation.'

'Other evidence?'

'Yes. It seems Ruff and Elita showed up *together* for the bail hearing in court this morning —'

'What's wrong with that? I'd expect them to attend the first hearing. And she's a probationer; she probably wanted to see how a bail hearing went...'

'Nothing wrong with that *intrinsically*. But the officer in the case — that's D.S. Myers of the robbery squad— he reported they were seen 'smiling' and 'joking' together down in cells near the Matron's office.'

I interjected: 'The implication being that if someone *smiles and jokes* with another person, they must be fucking each other?' I was irritated by the assumption.

'Why did D.S. Myers take time to report such an innocuous thing if it was innocent?' continued Beedi. 'I imagine because he thought that their conduct was inappropriate. And when this info is placed alongside a plausible report that suggests they probably stayed overnight at a hotel together, it seems their behaviour is less than innocent.'

'Well, it seems all *very* unlikely to me. Just a bunch of speculations and suspicions collected by filthy-minded men with over-active imaginations. These allegations are undoubtedly fueled by envy,' I told him.

'Whatever. That might be the case. The important thing is that we nip their behaviour in the bud. I want you to see both officers. Get accounts of what went happened last night. Make sure Ruff doesn't 'lean' on the Woman Constable, beforehand. You should interview her first.'

'Very well.'

'I want you to do it today.'

'Got it.'

'Let me have your written report by close-of-play.'

'Understood.'

———

I left Inspector Beedi's office feeling gutted. *What a grubby little Job this is.* My immediate point of view was that others had ganged-up on Ruff and Elita because they'd become resentful and jealous of them. My opinion was that Elita and Ruff's recent successes had shown the others up. Even the men on the Robbery Squad had an axe to grind. And so did the C.I.D.

Beedi had directed me to interview Elita first. But I had an alternative plan.

———

After a cup of Rosy Lee, I asked Wally West to take me for a ride in his Panda. We set out towards the edge of the town.

When we arrived at the post office near Ballymena Drive, I asked him to let me out of the car. I told him to collect me later from the same spot. I also asked him to keep my whereabouts secret. I tucked my 'civvie' jacket under my left arm, and my uniform tunic folded neatly on his back seat. 'I won't be longer than two hours —' I said 'I have got to see a man about a dog. Keep *shtum* for me, would you?'

Wally smiled, 'The betting shop is over there.' He pointed towards a dark doorway.

'Yes, I know,' I chuckled. 'See you later, alligator.'

Wally smiled and drove off.

———

I waited until the Panda was out of sight then pulled on my civilian jacket. I popped across the street then double-backed. Because I was *not* going to the betting shop.

I walked half a mile in the opposite direction.

Heading towards the police estate. And eventually, I arrived at Ruff's married quarters.

Because wanted to see Mrs. Palmerston.

62

Eve Palmerston came to the front door of the police house in her blue plastic work-coat. She produced a pleasant smile when she saw me: 'Clarence. How good of you to come. Come in. *Come in.* Everything is all right, isn't it?'

'Nothing to worry about Eve,' I told her.

I stepped into the house and brushed my boots on the coconut matting.

'Can I get you a tea?' she said. 'Or something stronger, maybe?'

'Tea is fine Mrs. P.' I strolled into the living room and sat on the couch. I admired her Swiss cheese plant before I flicked through a copy of Woman's Weekly found on the nest of tables.

'How are you now? After the accident?' Eve asked. She arrived with a mug of sweet tea. She sat as close as she could manage, with her cute backside perched high on the arm of the sofa. She looked deep into my eyes. For a moment, I thought she might brush her fingers through my hair. Instead, she put her hand around her cup and gazed into the steam.

'I feel reasonable now,' I told her 'A few twinges, I suppose. My back aches at night. And I got punched in the kidneys the other day. And it kind of knocked me for six...'

'Yes, I heard. Poor boy, Ruff told me.' Eve messed with the top of my hair. 'You need to see a masseuse,' she said.

'Do I?'

'I know a girl, a trained masseuse. She lives on the police estate. Mandy is her name. Her hubby works in the Collator's office at Barnet. She does massages *professionally*. Does them at her gaff where it's convenient and discreet. She's even got a proper massage table and the essential oils. Her old man doesn't mind. He lets her get on with it.'

'Really? She sounds good.'

'I can give you Mandy's number,' Eve said, with a twinkle. 'A good rub will do you good.'

I felt my face going red, so I changed the subject: 'Anyway…' I shuffled my feet. 'I thought I'd come around for a chat — I wanted to see how you were. Both of you that is. See what's happening. Find out how you're *both* getting on.'

'Getting on?'

'Well, you might remember, you told me that Ruff had been sleeping in his car. You suggested that things were not entirely perfect. In your marital relationship, I mean…'

'Yes. Ruff is *still* sleeping in his car.'

'Is he?'

'Things improved a bit. I admit. He doesn't smell so bad. He drinks less. He's even cut down on ciggies, he started to shave regular and clip his toenails and nose hair. And he even has a bath once a week…'

'Things have improved?'

'Yes. It's the fancy bint, I think. Whatsername? She's been a good influence on him.'

'Elita? She's been a *good* influence?'

'Yes, that's the fancy madam's name. Give the lass her due — she's straightened him out. He washes under-his-arms before he goes to work now. He never used to do that. He changes his underwear too. Sometimes twice a week. He doesn't smell like a rat. That's a real improvement, isn't it? And, as I said, he's cut down on booze and almost stopped smoking fags.'

'But he's still sleeping in the car? Why would he sleep in the car if you let him come back to bed? You say he doesn't stink anymore?'

'Well, I don't know. He's come to bed occasionally. But last night, for example, he didn't come to bed.'

'Oh. I am sorry to hear that.'

'He must have been working late...' she continued.

'That must be it,' I intervened. 'Ruff nicked two horrible ugly bastards for armed robbery.'

'Frankly, I don't want to know anything about it. Police wives do not like to talk about the possibility of threat that their husbands get themselves into. We know they get into all kinds of scrapes, but we ignore the possibility that they might get hurt, to keep our stress levels down.'

'Sorry. I didn't mean to distress you. But anyway, they were out extremely late...'

'They?'

'Ruff and Elita.'

'That must be it, then,' Eve said. 'What, did they both have the arrest?'

'Yup.'

'That's why he slept in the car,' she said. She twiddled fingers in her hair 'Because he didn't want to disturb me when he got home late.'

'That must be it' I agreed. 'How do you know that he slept in his car?' I had to ask this supplemental question to be sure.

'He came in and showered this morning. I heard the front door unlock. Then the shower being used. After that, I heard his old banger start-up and rumble down the road. It was around eight. Why do you ask?'

'No reason. Simply curious. But that doesn't prove that he slept in his car, does it?'

'No. I suppose not. But where did he sleep if it wasn't his car? Are you suggesting he slept on a park bench or out in the gutter?'

'No, nothing like that...'

'There is something wrong, isn't there?' she asked. 'You lied to me before. And I can see the same look in your face right now. I recognise the lying eyes. What are you hiding?'

'Nothing. Nothing at all.' I took Eve's hand into mine and squeezed her fingers. 'Everything is fine,' I said.

She stared at me with suspicion. 'What do you think of this fancy bint then? The new woman Constable?' Eve probed deep into my eyes. 'Do you like her?'

'I think she's very talented...'

'And beautiful?'

'Yes. Beautiful too,' I agreed.

Mrs. Palmerston kneaded my palm. 'More beautiful than me?'

I looked back awkwardly. She *had* me. She held my hand and continued to gaze. She attempted to detect lie-signs. What a smart little police-wife she was. 'She's *different* to you —' I suggested. I gulped for some air, 'She is graceful. Charming. But you're a fine-looking woman. You are a fully developed woman — if you don't mind me saying so. But Elita, well she is a mere girl.'

Eve Palmerston beamed back. 'Oh, thank you, Clarence. That's very noble of you. But, but I —'

'What?'

'I thought you and her — Elita and you—you might be seeing each other. You might be an item...' She snatched her hand quickly away. Then twisted a strand of her hair, dispassionately. 'Not that I mind. Of course.'

'Seeing each other. Elita and I? Whatever gave you that idea?'

'Well it makes sense, doesn't it? You are both educated. Both refined. Ruff describes you both as 'Ritzy', and he says she talks about you all the time. It makes sense you will probably hitch-up. Made for each other, you are. Both the same social class. A perfect match.'

'I haven't even thought about it...' I lied. 'She's a young probationary Constable, and I'm a sergeant. That could never work. And anyway, the Job wouldn't allow it. A Sergeant is not allowed to have an affair with a Constable.'

'Well that's good then,' Eve said.

'Is it?'

'Yes. Otherwise, I might be an incy-wincy bit green with envy.' With those words, she clouted me — playfully — on the shoulder.

I got up to leave. I placed my mug on the coffee table. 'Thanks for the drink Mrs. P.'

'Any time my love.' She pecked me on the cheek.

'Oh, before I go. One last thing —' I needed to get something off my mind: 'Are you still thinking of moving back to the West Midlands? You told me once you wanted to get Ruff to go back home.'

'Yes. Though now Ruff is more determined than ever to stay in London. This fancy new Plonk has given him a fresh lease of life. He's more alive than ever. He tells me he'll stay in the Met for good. I don't think he'll ever leave.'

'But you still want him to leave? Don't you? To return to the Midlands with you?'

'Yes, of course I do. I want to settle down and have babies. I would do anything to get him to leave the Force and come back home with me. We can't go on like this, you see. We can't raise a family on thirty-eight pounds a week. Most of which, incidentally, goes on booze and fags.'

'If there's anything I can do to help you will let me know, yes? Maybe I can have a chat with Ruff. Get him to see sense.'

'I doubt it will do any good. But it might be worth a try. Thank you.'

'You're welcome,' I said.

Eve scribbled some numbers onto a notelet in the hallway. She tucked the fold of paper into my shirt pocket and gave me another kiss.

'What's this?' I asked as I patted my pocket.

'Mandy's number. Get your body over to her massage bed. Let her give you the ride of your life. You won't be sorry.'

'Thanks,' I said. 'I might just do that...'

63

After refreshments, I slipped into the back of the blue Rover.

Elita sat in the wireless operator's position, by Ruff's side. We purred out of the station yard and into the High Street. 'You've had a busy day...' I said, employing a deliberate air of spontaneous indifference.

'We went to court,' Ruff explained 'To the bail hearing. The court rejected bail. So, the scum-bags are locked away at Her Majesty's pleasure for the foreseeable...'

'You must be cream-crackered,' I muttered. 'The pair of you, right? What time did you get home last night?'

Elita glanced at Ruff before she answered: 'Just after two a.m. It was a long shift. We went with the Sweeney to grab the outstanding suspect...'

'Good gracious...' I said. 'That's very late. So you couldn't go and celebrate?'

'Funny you should say that,' Elita spelt it out: 'We talked about getting a drink at a fleabag hotel Ruff knows that serves 'afters' — I didn't feel like it, so I went home...'

'Really?'

'I had to get up at the crack of dawn to muck out the horses. Then off to court with Rufus...' She mussed Ruff's ginger hair as she said it. 'A girl's work is never done.'

'Quite,' Ruff grunted.

Well, that's *that* then. I thought. *Case closed.*

While the Rover rumbled happily and gracefully into the High Street, we were prompted into motivation by the booming voice of M.P. on the main-set radio. 'All units, all units, Quebec Mike section and all units 'Q Quebec'. Police Officer requires urgent assistance. Repeat, *urgent assistance.* 12 High Street. Quebec Mike. Units to respond?'

Elita accepted the emer-call. We were seconds from that address. Ruff thumbed-on the rooftop beacon while Elita activated the two-tone horns as she wrote down the details of the call in her R/T log.

We approached the centre of the main street and saw a commotion. There was a sense of confusion as shoppers gathered near a tobacco shop. A man waved wildly, beckoning us over. He pointed at a shop entrance. We came to a halt, and Elita was first out of the car. Ruff was out quickly too, and running before I had even opened my door.

I caught up with the officers at the shop. I saw a pool of blood and a uniformed Constable on the floor. He appeared crushed, demoralized and cut down. His head was held by a twenty-something brown-haired girl. 'I'm a nurse...' she told all-and-sundry. It seemed the lad's nose had been broken. He'd been knocked senseless. It took me a while to recognize who the officer was because of the blood and snot. I finally acknowledged it to be young Peter Prince.

'Peter? Who did this to you?' I shouted. 'We need to get the fucker...' Elita crouched and wiped our young Constable's forehead. This action revitalized him. 'Anyone called an ambulance yet?' I shouted. The man who'd waved-us-in gave the nod. 'I called 999. You got here quick...' he said.

'Did you see what happened?' I asked.

'Yes. The young officer stopped a vehicle. A gold Daimler, I believe. After he finished with the man, the young constable entered the shop. He left the driver and the car by the road. But the driver of the Daimler followed the P.C. into the shop and beat him up. The driver was tall and thin. Over six feet, I guess. Wearing a blue suit.'

'Why?' I asked Peter Prince. 'Why did he thump you?'

'Sarge. I stopped the Daimler because it looked well iffy. I asked the geezer for a bit of identification so I could make a few checks on him and his jam-jar. He handed me his licence. Maybe to shut-me-up. I went to use the phone in the shop. To do the checks, you know, on his name and licence plate using the free-phone number they gave out at Hendon. But the geezer demanded his licence back. He even tried to snatch it out of my hand. I wouldn't let him have the licence, so he punched me.'

'Good God Peter Where's your personal radio?'

'There were no bats left in the cage. The last personal radio had been taken out by Inspector Beedi. He said I ought to come back later to see if any bat-phones had been returned...'

'This is rifuckulous — ' I said. 'How are officers expected to do this pony job without radios?' We heard klaxons as the ambulance approached.

'Where's the gold Daimler now?' Ruff asked. 'We need to get the fucker who did this to your boat race.'

'It drove off, Ruff. It drove towards the direction of Park Drive.'

'I got the registration mark — ' a witness offered. 'It's MMX 555.'

'Good lad,' said Ruff, grabbing the hand-written note from the man. 'Right, there's not much time. We'll have a scout around the patch. Try to find the shit who did this. He can't have gotten far.'

The cavalry were still turning up because I hadn't cancelled other units: 'M.P. M.P. Cancel any further to Quebec Mike High Street. Officer located. There's no need for additional. Instead, please circulate the following index: Mike, Mike X-ray Five, Five, Five. Believed a gold-coloured Daimler. The occupier of this jam-jar is responsible for the assault on Old Bill.'

'Received.'

I found Wally West in the middle of the crowd. He stood in amongst the shocked faces that gazed in silence at the stricken officer. It's not often you see a Copper on the floor with blood all over his *mush.* 'Wally, take care of Peter. Go in the grumbulance with him. We are going after the Anthony Blunt who did this to him.' As I said these words, I glanced at the nurse. She seemed discernibly peeved by the Cockney expletives I had been using: 'Scuse my French, love,' I told her. 'But I'm fuming mad about the evil fuckwad who did this...' She nodded.

Ruff, Elita and I pushed through the crowd and returned to the area car. We roared off.

'I have an idea ...' Ruff said.

'I knew he would —' Elita commented, a glint of admiration in her eyes.

64

Ruff drove the wireless-car to the open-spaces. 'I know a 'cut' near the recreation ground that the old lags use...' he explained. 'They leave getaway cars by the alleyway and run through it. They use the 'cut' after a robbery or hold-up...'

The area car roared towards the dead end. Sure enough, as we approached, we detected the unmistakable rear end of a Daimler Sovereign parked by the public land. 'You're a genius Ruff, my love,' Elita said, as she inspected the index mark and made sure it matched the one, we'd been given earlier. We pulled in behind the iffy motor and Elita informed M.P. we had located the suspect vehicle. Ruff jumped from our motor to take a look about: checking the heat of the bonnet and inspecting the tyres. That's when I heard a squawked and confused noise coming from Elita. It that reminded me of a parrot who'd gone Radio Rental. I saw Elita drop the main-set microphone and toss her message log into the foot-well. Then she smashed the car door open and pushed her long legs out: 'Sergeant —' she shouted. 'He's on the run...'

Before I reacted — Elita was off on her pins. Legging across the open space at the end of 'the cut'. I did my best to follow in her gigantic footsteps — but my back gave me hell. All I could do was jog at a pathetic pace. I sensed Ruff wheezing-along behind me, but I didn't pause or turn around.

In the distance — beyond the sports pitches — I spied a tall man running at a steady rate towards a row of garden fences. At that stage, he was a long way off. There was no chance we'd ever catch him. On the other hand, *perhaps Elita could succeed in running him down.*

I stopped for a breather and bent my head to catch a lungful.

'She'll not catch him — he's too far off,' Ruff said, as he put a warm hand on the flat of my back and gasped for air. 'Mind you, look at her go. She's like a fucking gazelle.' We admired her long-legged form as she rushed over the muddy grass. Her ponytail shone in the afternoon light. 'Oh shit,' cried Ruff. 'I hope she *doesn't* catch the fucker. She couldn't, could she? He's a big ugly brute, and he'll murder her. He'll do a lot of damage to a woman. You saw what he did to Peter Prince. Oh shit, she's gaining on him...' We both watched, helpless, as the large man began to slow while Elita made up ground.

'Come on — we'd better jog-on. Elita might need help if that evil bastard turns around and has a go...'

Ruff started to run again, and I did my best to keep up, but it was agony. Soon I had to halt again, to gaze simply. The criminal turned around and, as I feared, he looked as if he was about to deal with Elita who had almost caught up. I sensed the man summarized his options. *This could turn very nasty,* I thought.

Then, out of the corner of my eye, I glimpsed a small black speck. At first, I thought I'd imagined it — but no — there was undoubtedly a black bullet zooming towards the man. It travelled at enormous speed. I rubbed my eyes to see better, then became adequately aware of what was happening. In my dull-witted state, I realized the *black speck* was, in fact, a dog. The dog hurtled towards the fugitive.

With difficulty, I tried to focus on the dog and saw yet another form, further-away, jogging behind. This was the form of a policeman wearing a cap.

'Good grief,' I said to myself. 'What a stroke of luck.'

Within seconds the dog-shaped *speck* had reached the villain. I watched with immense satisfaction as the animal pulled the man to the ground. The baddie was quickly bitten into submission. A few moments later, Elita reached the suspect. Perceptive as ever — she stood at arm's length and waited — while the dog 'did his thing.' And, quite soon after that, the handler made his way to them both.

By the time I got to the scene, the Dog Handler had the prisoner in a headlock while the police dog snapped at the bad-man's feet. Ruff stood beside Elita and held her shoulders: 'You're under arrest for assault occasioning actual bodily harm,' Elita told the suspect. The man's arm had been savagely torn.

'That was a stroke of luck,' I said to the handler.

'Yes. I was walking my dog on the playing fields when I saw your Plonk sprinting after this shithead. May I introduce police dog, Trinity? He's one quick fucker, isn't he? When I let him off his leash, he moved like a fucking missile. Did you see him go?'

'Yes, I did —' I said with a grin. 'It was a thing of pure beauty.'

65

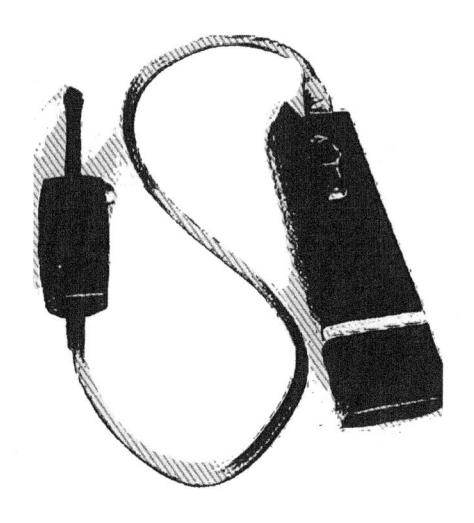

66

The Hale and the Hearty

Ruff's best pal, Constable Dave Yale, returned to work the following week.

He'd been 'Up North' on a rather lengthy break, investigating homes and finding himself a new job. Dave made an announcement at the card-table during morning refreshments: 'Folks, I've got big news...' The canteen went quiet. 'This time next month I will be in Cumberland. New job, new mortgage, new life...'

'What's wrong with your life here?' said old Godfrey Lambert as he ripped a raspberry tart so prodigious it was heard the other side of the large table.

'Good grief Godders... It's a miracle you didn't follow that through,' I remarked.

'If you like a lot of chocolate on your brisket, join our club,' sang Charlie M.C. Butler.

'Opening time is anytime' Godfrey uttered, in response.

'Seriously though —' continued 'Misty' Bill Winfield, turning to Dave Yale 'What will you do in Cumberland?'

'Where is Cumber Land anyhow?' interrupted young Peter Prince.

Ruff spat onto his next playing card and slammed it to his forehead. But everyone ignored him because they gazed at Dave instead, waiting for a response.

'Cumberland is located in the northwest of England,' Dave explained. 'It's close to Scotland. God's country. Houses are six grand...'

'Wow,' Godfrey exclaimed.

'I'm going to be a milkman up there. Already had my interview for the new job. Up at three o'clock. Home by midday. Forty hours a week. Steady pay. Nix stress. Improved money — plus a nice gaff, so me and the Trouble can bring a few bin-lids into the world...'

'Better money?'

'Improved. Fifty quid a week. Better than this firm, yes.'

'God.'

'You're hushed. Cat got your tongue?' Dave glared at Ruff.

'Sorry, mate. I will miss you...' admitted Ruff. 'But I can't get excited about this news. You know what I mean. I'm not excited because, well you know... It's not fair. It's *not right.*'

'What isn't right about it?'

'Because you're a good copper, Dave. You're one of the best. It's not right you've been forced into leaving the job. I can't get excited about that can I? I'm pleased for you, and your missus, of course, I am... but the world needs good coppers, doesn't it? So, this is a sad time mate. Not to be celebrated.'

Limbs shifted, and feet shuffled. Silence fell on the table.

'*Aye up!* There's fanny about —' someone shouted.

The tense atmosphere was provisionally boosted by a trio of delicious C.I.D. typists who teetered into the canteen for mid-morning toasties. 'I wouldn't mind putting a brisket in her basket,' Peter Prince announced, as he stared at the long-legged bint at the front of the queue, the one with red hair and substantial thrupenny bits. Peter made an obscene gesture with his fist.

'When Woodie the Woodpecker knocks, be sure to let him in,' sang Godfrey Lambert.

'It's amazing' what raisins can do —' Bill Winfield shouted, as he mimed the act of swaying an elongated penis in her general direction. Everyone snickered at this. Encouraged by the cheers, he thrust his hipbones at the girls and said, 'I like a lot of lipstick on my dipstick...'

'Gentlemen, *gentlemen* ...' Ruff cut in. His eyes were narrowed, his nostrils flared, and he was clearly bothered: 'Have we forgotten there's a lady present?'

'There's no need to fret over me love, I'm not upset,' Elita said.

'However —' persisted Ruff, ignoring her comment. 'The behaviour from these lads is childish —boorish.'

'Ruff, fuck that. We're just having a little giraffe, aren't we?' Peter remarked.

'Yeah. Bollocks to that Ruff. Why did you change?' Misty added.

'Yes, why did you change?' Dave whispered.

'What?' Ruff shouted. 'What did you fucking say?'

'Nothing.'

'I heard you say *something*, Dave. I thought you were my mate an' all... You asked me why I changed. Why do you think I fucking changed? I repeat: why do you think I changed?'

Dave wouldn't be led down a blind alleyway and into an argument, so took a sip of tea.

'I asked you a question —' Ruff barked. He narrowed his eyes some more: 'I asked *why do you think I've changed*?'

His best friend shrugged but wouldn't be drawn into a row.

'You are all living in the past,' Ruff declared as he looked around the table. 'This kind of conduct was fine back in '69. But it's 1975. Things are changing. Society has expanded. Women are now equal. They even work alongside us. It's about time you bunch stopped behaving like overgrown schoolboys who'd never seen a pair of Bristols in your life. The lot of you need to mature.' With these words, Ruff pushed back his chair, slammed his cards on the table, and made a dramatic move to go.

'Come on dear. Let's do some police work' he said to Elita. He put a protective hand around her shoulder.

'I've not finished my game, honey. You go. I'll catch-up when I'm done,' Elita gave a weak smile.

'Suit yourself,' Ruff grunted 'Do what you damn well please...'

He slammed the canteen the door as he marched off.

The ladies of the C.I.D. surveyed the incident with open-lipped wonder. 'Drama,' whispered one.

The mood settled once Ruff had departed. Dave suggested that maybe he ought to go outside and join Ruff for a ciggie and hug him.

'Leave it, Davey...' Elita told him. 'He's coming to terms with your departure. That's all. He's irritable because you announced you were going. I think he's afraid....'

'I feel guilty.'

'You shouldn't feel guilty, honey. You're doing the right thing. You're doing it for your wife and your family. Ruff will get over it.'

'Anyway. Who's coming to my leaving do?' Dave said with a smile. The question brought amused expressions to the faces around the table.

'When?' asked Godfrey.

'Thursday, at Quebec Bravo sports club. Seven until eleven. We got a disco too.'

'Great.'

'The evening before early turn...' groaned Peter.

'Yes. But it's the only day we are all available. Everyone welcome.'

'Smashing,' Elita said as she collected-up Ruff's cards to deal a fresh hand.

67

Bristol Cities

IMPORTED
IRISH
WHISKEY

OUR FINEST

68

Dave Yale's leaving do at the sports club was a bittersweet affair. None of us looked forward to saying goodbye. But we were pleased to see him off. So, we participated with a good heart and a generous nature. The entire team turned out for the bash. Inspector Beedi, wearing a black-tie ensemble, told everyone: 'I have to nip off smartish to a Lodge function, so I can't stay to make a speech.'

What a spineless bastard he'd turned out to be.

Even that nob Fart'n Mart'n turned up at the 'do'. He walked through the club doors in a Starsky & Hutch jumper and circulated the function room, making small talk with wives and girlfriends. Like me, Beedi and Fart'n Mart'n *hadn't* brought along any company. Neither had Elita.

When Elita walked into the room, she wore a minimalistic drape-gown, and all eyes were upon her. Shiny high-heeled boots complemented her lengthy legs and rounded off a vision of true splendour. I watched Elita prowl the place like a panther. I sensed she preferred older men in the group. She offered syrupy smiles to women and polite nods to younger guys. But saved her most sumptuous eye-contact for the older fellows. Finally, she reached Ruff. He pecked her on the cheek, so she smiled back and gave him a playful slap. She bent her knee towards his thigh, and flirtatiously lifted her, arm to smooth long hair and expose an exquisitely nude armpit.

'Cheeky little sweetheart, isn't she?'

I whirled on my heels to see who'd commented. The words came from Eve Palmerston or, more appropriately, Mrs. Ruff.

'Hi Mrs. P. I didn't see you creeping up. How are you?'

Mrs. Palmerston concentrated her attention back on Elita. 'Look at those come-hither eyelashes...' she hissed. 'That girl is all flicker and frisk. A proper little sex kitten.'

'What, oh Elita you mean?' I verbalized, pretending I didn't know what she meant. 'Yeah, she knows how to work an audience I suppose...'

'Don't expect me to believe you hadn't noticed,' Eve Palmerston said with a knowing smile. 'I saw your jaw drop the moment she stepped into the room...'

'Really, Mrs. P? You saw my jaw drop?' I felt my cheeks redden. 'It was that obvious?'

'Yup.'

'Anyway, how are you, my love?' I asked, pulling my eyes from Elita.

'Could be better Clarence...' Eve said. 'I wish it was Ruff and me moving up North. Ruff is cut up about his mate's departure, of course, but now he's surer than sure he'll stay down South in the Job for the foreseeable future.'

'I see.'

'Well, aren't you going to go over and make a play for her?'

'What?'

'Aren't you going to go over and save that poor girl from my awful husband? Make a play for her?'

'Oh, right. Yes, *yes*. I'll go over and do that right now.'

'Good to see you, Clarence. Let's chat later.'

'Okeydokey,' I said. I made my way towards Elita, as directed by Ruff's wife.

As I approached Elita, the girl flicked her ponytail my way and glanced carelessly, even superficially, in my *general* direction. The superficial look she gave shattered my impulse. I was about to walk away, to divert to the bar, when I heard my name being called: 'Clarence, *here*.' Elita's luminous smile and lively eyes concentrated on me. 'Come' she said, with a beckoning wave. She slapped her lap as if communicating with a gundog. 'I was telling Ruff about the armed robbers we nicked,' she went on, 'They put their hands-up to three other blags. So, the Flying Squad want to give us a commendation for it. That's great, isn't it?'

'Yes, it is...' I muttered. 'But we shouldn't be talking about Job right here, right now. It's bad form. The 'other halves' don't appreciate it. Also, it's not fair on Dave and his Missus.

'Oh...' said Elita. 'I hadn't thought of that.'

The void was filled with Dave's timely approach.

'Sargey, hello. Hello Elita. Have you both got drinks? What do you think of the disco? Nice frock by the way, love.' He couldn't stop staring down Elita's bold cleavage.

'Thank you, Davey,' Elita said, modestly. She planted a kiss on his cheek then held onto his arm. Dave's Missus, Cleo, turned up and looked at them together with resentment.

'You haven't met my trouble and strife, have you?' Dave went on. 'Let me introduce you to her...'

Feeling out-classed and up-staged by the spry crumpet that hung onto her husband's arm, Mrs. Cleo Yale — who looked beautiful in a shimmering green caftan, by the way — gave the young woman police constable a cold hand and the deepest glower she could manage. Her expression meant: 'leave my man alone, hussy.'

Dave and his wife went to circulate, and Elita put her arm around Ruff's waist to steady herself. 'I don't think Cleo likes me much,' she breathed.

'I shouldn't worry, jelly-bean.' he told her. 'This is the first and last time you'll see Cleo. She's off to Cumberland at the weekend. Never to return.'

'Are you helping Dave with the move?' I asked.

'Can't get time off...' Ruff muttered. 'His brother in law is coming down to help.'

'But you'll get a chance to say a personal farewell I assume?'

'Don't know. Maybe. Maybe not. I won't have time.'

'Never Can Say Goodbye' started to be played on the disco-floor.

'Coming to dance, Clarence?' Elita inquired, with shameless forwardness. She moved her limbs to the supple rhythms as I watched the rippled motion of her super-fit body.

'Me?' I asked, somewhat surprised by her offer.

'Go for it —' Ruff said as if he needed to bestow consent.

Elita gave a cheeky smile and took my hand. We went to the dance floor. I'm sure every bloke in the room watched us and thought: *What a lucky blighter* while they leered at her curves. On the uncarpeted area, I moved Elita around so I could spy on Mrs. Palmerston. I'd hoped she was going to be attended by Ruff. But he lingered near the bar, cigarette in one hand, pint pot on the other, with his back facing his Missus. He started yakking to the barmaid.

I saw Eve sat on a velvet cushioned bench alongside that ignorant shit-head Charlie 'M.C.' Butler. He'd parked himself beside her and blew cigarette smoke into her eyes. I felt torn. It was impossible to be in two places at once; I wanted to go and save Eve Palmerston. But on the other hand, I wished to give Elita the attention she deserved.

'You seem distracted...' Elita shouted, over the disco groove.

'Sorry love,' I said. 'Just looking around the room.'

She nodded, so we continued to dance. But Elita sensed my heart wasn't in it. Once Gloria Gaynor finished, she patted my bum and made her way back to Ruff.

I felt slightly crestfallen but decided to cheer myself up by chatting with Eve. As I approached the velvet bench, exactly where she'd been sitting moments earlier, I realized she'd run off.

She headed towards the bar area. I sprinted after. She had burst into tears. What had that scoundrel Constable M.C. Butler been telling her?

―――

I watched the drama unfold.

Eve rushed to the bar. She pulled the beer-mug from her husband's clammy hand and threw a pint of ale straight into his bloodshot eyes. Then, before he was able to react, she drew-back a closed fist and threw a punch. Her knuckles hit Ruff straight in the snotter. His nose burst-open in a spray of blood and mucus. Satisfied, she walked away, wiping her hands on the front of her frock. She even took a well-aimed jab at Elita as she passed. The Constable dodged the right-hook just in time. Her punch missed Elita's cheek by a gnat's whisker.

As Mrs. Ruff hurried from the venue, tears welled in her eyes.

'Wait here...' directed Dave Yale to his pal. He patted Ruff on the shoulders and tugged at my arm. 'Let's go and get her.'

We rushed after Eve Palmerston. She'd already made it out of the club and into the car park. She pulled open the door of her husband's decrepit, rust-bucket, Hillman Imp and had flicked down the sun visor to allow the hidden car-keys to plunk into her lap. After a jiggle, she managed to fire up the crappy engine. She cranked the gearstick into first as Dave and I emerged into the lot, to see the banger pootle out of the clubhouse side road and into the public thoroughfare.

'Bugger,' said Dave. 'We weren't quick enough to grab her...' He pointed at his yellow Ford Capri. 'Let's go after her in that...' We ran to his Capri and jumped in. Then we began our pursuit.

It did not take long to find her.

Mrs. Palmerston had travelled less than a half-mile down the backroad before her car had rolled off the highway. The front wheels had trundled in to a deep ditch. The engine was still running when we arrived.

I went to the driver's door: 'Come on, I'll tug you out,' I said to Eve, as I forced open the mangled door and pulled her shoulder from the heap.

'Come to nick me, have you?' she shouted. 'Going to be nicked for drunk-drive, am I?' Her spit speckled my face, and her eyes were inflamed.

'We're here to rescue you,' remarked Dave as he inspected the damage. 'One wheel punctured, smashed headlights. Doors crumpled.'

'Come on...' screamed Eve. She put her wrists out to be hand-cuffed. 'Take me in then you pair of nonces. Fucking nick me. Come on. Read me the Judges Rules.' Dave put his jacket around her shoulders and led her up the muddy bank. 'I need to be arrested...' she continued. 'Nick me. *Nick me.* Assault, drink-drive. T.D.A. Take me down the road. Sling me in a cell. That's all I'm good for...'

'Hush now,' Dave told her.

'Add attempted assault to the charge-list. Because I tried to smack that fucking bitch *too*. I'll put my hands up in court. Write that in your fucking pocketbooks, you pair of fucking twats...'

'We'll have the night shift put a rope around the car...' Dave replied, blandly. 'Haul it out the ditch. They can tow it back home with the van.'

Mrs. Palmerston started to weep oversized tears.

'What did he tell you?' I asked. I offered Eve my hankie for a snuffle, 'What did constable M.C. Butler say that made you go mad?'

'Constable Butler,' she said, between bleats. 'He said Ruff and fancy-pants had spent the night together. In some trashy hotel. Just the other night. He said it was common knowledge, all around the station. All around the neighbourhood.' I rubbed Eve's shoulders as she took a slim cigarette from her purse and lit it. Her hands trembled as she spoke: 'I do not know what's worse... The fact that my old man has been over the side. Or the fact that I have been publicly humiliated.'

'It's not true,' I told her. 'Butler is a shit-stirrer. He has an overactive imagination. He's a nasty troublemaker. He told you that lie to get a reaction...'

'It's not true? I saw them by the bar. Grinning and giggling. Swapping kisses. Don't tell me he's not fucking her. Of course, he is. Once he'd told me, I could see things clear as day. Ruff hasn't given me one moment of his time. Not tonight nor any night. He's spent all his time with *her*. I feel so foolish... But I didn't guess... I didn't guess.' She began to sob again.

'But Elita does that with *all* the men. Didn't you see? She's a prick-teaser, plain and simple. Do you think she would fuck your Ruff? Think about it a moment. Would she? She's a class-act, isn't she? She could grab *any* man she wanted... So why would she go for your great galumphing knob of a husband?'

Mrs. Palmerston remained silent. I could see her mull things over.

'Would Ruff go over the side?' asked Dave. 'He might be tempted. But would he *actually* do it?'

'Think about it...' I pushed on 'What woman would have Ruff? He's overweight, out of condition, belligerent and oafish. He drinks like a catfish, smokes like a chimney-dick and sweats like a hippo-beast in a sauna. He's not exactly a male-model, is he?'

Eve Palmerston smiled at this last comment. 'But how do you know?' she asked, 'How do you know he isn't shagging? He might be bored with our marriage. Surely he wouldn't turn down the chance of sex-booty from a beauty like *her* when offered on a plate?'

'Well, first off, sex-booty was *not* offered on a plate. I know that for a fact. Elita might be fond of your hubby, but she's not interested in screwing him. She has *standards*. She told me that herself. Secondly, and perhaps more importantly, Ruff would unquestionably turn down sex booty if it was offered... Because he's in love *with you*. You're his old lady. His old china. He would *never* stray.'

Those words convinced her, and she began to blubber loudly.

This time Eve's tears were more convincing less aggrieved. 'What have I done Clarence?' she asked between sobs. I rubbed her shoulders. 'I'm sorry. Dave, ' she continued. 'Sorry, I ruined your party. Oh, God, I'm sorry. What happens now? '

69

The Gary Player

The next morning the mood on Early Turn was extremely subdued.

The officers got on with their work quietly and unobtrusively. It seemed fortuitous that the Godfrey Lambert had resumed from his well-earned annual leave and was able to drive the wireless car once again. It meant that Ruff and Elita could be 'divided' — so I posted Ruff to the van.

There was a sense of calm once he'd made the tea. The officers fanned hot cups then sipped the sweet brew. Subsequently, the units led-off from the station yard and into the working day.

———

Inspector Beedi called me in to see him just after lunch. He said, over the bat-phone, that he *needed a word pronto*. I passed Sergeant Paddy Gallaher in the hallway, on my way to the Inspector's office. 'Patience and tolerance, young man...' he said, with a wise nod. 'Accept the inevitable and move on. That's my advice.' *What did he mean?*

When I arrived at Inspector Beedi's door, he motioned me to

come in right away. I closed the door behind. Before I could take a seat, he handed me a sheet of type-written paper. I recognized it as the kind of form that's used in police disciplinary investigations to notify an officer of an allegation. It's known as a Form 163. I read the main body of the document in silence: 'It is alleged that during the summer of 1975, your conduct fell short of what is expected of an officer.' I looked up at the Inspector, but he indicated that I should read it all. 'During the stated period (1) You were seen in a public place — with a married officer — and were seen to be 'happy' and 'laughing' together (2) You visited a licensed premises with the same police officer, and you shared a drink together (3) You attended an official function with the same officer — even though you were aware that other officers would see you at the same function and the function was at a licensed premises (4) This behaviour — when each incident is taken together — constitutes behaviour that is likely to bring the force into disrepute.'

I looked at Beedi. He remained expressionless.

It was only after the second reading that I realized the Form 163 was *intended for Elita*. The recipient on the top was addressed to Constable Elita du Maurier.

'This is for Elita?'

'Yup.'

'Why her? What's she done wrong?'

'The allegations are on the Form.'

'What do you want me to say?'

'I don't want you to say anything. Just serve the 163 on her that's all. And write a note in your Pocket Book.'

'What?'

'You heard.'

'Why don't you serve the bloody form? Why me?'

'Because you are the Section Sergeant.'

I studied the form again and started to feel my blood boil.

'This is fucking balls,' I said. 'I'm not serving *this* on her. It's a bloody joke.'

'If you don't serve this form, I'll get Paddy Gallaher to do it.'

'He knows about this?'

'Yes. Of course, he *does*. I discuss *everything* with him.'

'What if I refuse to serve it and *he* does it instead?'

'As I say, Sergeant Gallaher will do my bidding. And you will be stuck-on. Disciplinary action for failing to comply with a lawful order. Do you want to think about it?'

I folded the Form and placed it into my top pocket.

'Right. I'll serve it,' I said. 'You leave me no choice. But I want you to know I'm feeling pretty fucking riled about this.'

'I thought you might be...' Inspector Beedi replied, with just the hint of a grin. 'This makes up for all the times Ruff has had me over, and *you* have failed to live up to my expectations...'

I stepped out of the office without saying another word. But at that moment I could have happily strangled the blighter.

70

I called Elita on the bat-phone and told her to meet me in the snooker room.

I explained that Godfrey Lambert should come along to the snooker room too. I was not surprised to find that Ruff showed up 'just in time' to help. I told him to wait in the canteen until I was ready to see him. He gave me an odd stare as if he could tell *something was up* so I told him I would brief him after I spoke with Elita. He nodded.

'What's this all about, Skipper?' Constable Lambert asked once Ruff had wandered off.

'I'll be with you in a tick, darling,' I told Elita who gave me an unguarded smile as she entered the snooker room. 'I want to give Godfrey the low-down — I'll be right with you.'

'Okey-dokey artichokey,' she said.

Once she was out of sight, I turned to Godfrey: 'Would you object to acting as *her* 'police friend'? I am about to serve Elita with a Form 163.'

'She might prefer Ruff to act as her friend,' he suggested. 'I think he's a better mate to her than I might be...'

'That's true —I know she might prefer that. But it would suit *me* better if Ruff was kept out of this, at least for now. Do you get me?'

'What is it then?'

'It's best you find out when I tell Elita and not before. At this point, I'm just wondering if you are willing to accompany the officer into the room while she's being served with the notice.'

'Fine by me.'

'Thanks, Godfrey, I owe you.'

We took the walk together; he lit his pipe and took a puff while I cracked my knuckles.

Elita was seated by the billiards table as we entered. She was no fool — she knew something was up — but looked composed, nonetheless. Godfrey glanced at her with fellow feeling and took a chair alongside. I rested my butt on the edge of the cloth. 'Elita. I have been asked to serve you with a notice. It's a form 163. Under regulations, you are entitled to have a 'police friend' present when I serve the notice. 'A friend' means a person chosen by you to be an impartial advice-giver. My recommendation is that you use Godfrey as a friend. Though, if you don't want him, that's fine too. Do you want Godfrey to stay here and witness this as your friend?'

Elita dropped her chin in surprise, and her eyes went wide. She took a moment to grab a breath. 'You are bound to be anxious,' I added, while she pinched her eyebrows with her long fingers. 'That's why it's good to have a friendly face here with you.'

'I see. I'm happy to have Godfrey. Though I would prefer Ruff. Isn't that something that we can arrange? If not, I trust you, and Godders, you both know what's best for me...'

I took the form 163 from my tunic pocket, unfolded it, and passed it to her to read. She took the paper and read it in silence. Once she'd done so, she passed it to Godfrey. He read it and handed it back.

'If this is some kind of joke — it's in rather poor taste,' she declared. 'If it's *not* a joke — if this is bloody serious—I will get my Dad's lawyer on the case. Our barrister will give *you lot* a bloody good whacking. And when our family barrister is finished grinding you and the Inspector into the dirt, you'll both be looking for other careers while you pay me compensation for the rest of your sad, pitiful lives. So, all that said, I'm hoping this is a wind-up...'

'I'm sorry, Elita. It's no wind-up.'

'It says I was 'happy' and 'laughing' — what kind of shit is that? Surely, it's not a crime to be happy in a public place? Not even under the Police Regulations...'

I shook my head because I felt discouraged and defeated.

'They are not out to get *you*, Miss,' Godfrey said, tapping his pipe against the snooker table. 'It's Ruff they want. They're *using* you to get to him. They want Ruff's scalp, see, and this is the way they intend to get it...'

'They do?'

'Yes. They have wanted him for yonks. Now, it seems, they've got him by the dangly bits. You're the weak link, see? They get him by getting you. They hope he will over-react and make a big bloody scene and they'll have him where they want him.'

'I'll bloody show them how weak I can be. I'm the weakest link, am I? I will take them to the Industrial Tribunal,' Elita huffed and threw her arms into the air. 'I'll take them to the bloody cleaners.'

'Listen to Godfrey,' I told her. 'He's providing good counsel. This isn't about *you*. It's about Ruff. Don't you see? The Inspector is using you as bait.'

'What should I do?'

'We will get this whole thing turned around, I'm sure of it. So you are left in the clear. Then you can get on with your police career. That's the most important outcome, isn't it?'

'Really? Is that what you *really* think? What about Ruff? He has more police service than I have. He's more valued. Wouldn't you prefer to rally around him and dump me? I am the probationer, after all...'

'Ruff's way past any help now, Miss.' Godfrey said. 'If they don't get him today, they'll get him tomorrow. Or the day after. It's only a matter of time before they shaft him. Meanwhile, you've got a whole career ahead of you... and that's something worth saving...'

'You would lose Ruff to save a girl?' she questioned. 'Both of you? You would both support me, a mere girl, at the cost of Ruff?'

'You're not *any* girl though, are you?' I whispered. 'You're exceptional. You will be a Detective Superintendent one day. I'm sure of it. And what's to become of Ruff? Even if he survives this shit, there will be more around the corner. He'll be facing another calamity within a week, mark my words. His toilet at home is literally wall-papered with Form 163's. Even if he survives this one, somehow, there'll be many more... he'll only ever amount to Constable, on shift —' Elita looked into my eyes and sighed. 'Ruff should return home. Home to the Midlands, where he belongs. With a loving wife. Where he can start a new life. That's what is needed now. And *you* can make it happen.'

'What do you want me to do?' Elita asked.

71

The Tin Tack

'You told me once that you wanted to start a new life in the North,' I told Ruff when I found him sitting alone in the station canteen.

We sipped milky coffees. 'Your old lady wants bin lids...' I explained. 'But she can't afford to have 'em on police pay. You will inevitably return to the Black Country one day and help manage the laundromat business with your in-laws. You know that day is coming, so why put it off any longer?'

'Why are you telling me this?' he said. 'What's this all about Skipper?'

'Is it true? Do you love your wife enough to return to the Midlands? To leave the Job?'

'I want to stay here...'

'I know you do. But what if your marriage was on the rocks? What if it was last chance saloon? One last chance to do the right thing by her, by your missus? Your last opportunity to save your marriage?'

'She walloped me last night. She thinks I'm helping myself to the nookie jar. She thinks I'm tupping Elita.'

'Well, have you? Have you been giving it one, I mean?'

'No. of course I bloody haven't.' He gazed at me with his pink-lashed eyes. 'You know perfectly well I wouldn't.'

'But you love her, yes?'

'What?' He peered at his pack of cigarettes on the tabletop.

'You love her?' I repeated. 'Love my Missus? Is that what you're asking?'

'You know what I'm asking mate, so stop evading the question. Do you love *her*?'

'For fuck's sake, Sarge —' Ruff avoided the question again but made shifting movements to leave.

'Do you love Elita? Yes or no?'

'Shit, man. This is awkward. I haven't touched her — if that's what you're asking. I haven't laid a finger. She's a classy girl. And that's why I respect her so much. She's going to be a fine copper. Her Mum and Dad are upstanding citizens. I have a high opinion of her. There, will that do?'

'*No*. That will not do. I asked you a particular question. And I need a straight answer. I need it *right now*. Do you love Elita?'

'Yes,' he nodded. He tumbled his cigarette lighter over-and-over in his clumsy fingers. 'But that means nothing. I love my old lady too. I love her more,' he added.

'Do you? Do you really love your old lady more than you love Elita?'

'Yes. Yes, of course I fucking do. For fuck's sake, Sarge. Leave it out, will you? I feel uneasy about all this love-talk and shit. It's not *manly* to be going on about love. Where is the chat leading anyways?'

I pulled the folded Form 163 from my tunic pocket and handed it over.

Ruff took the paper and read it for a moment. Then folded it in silence and handed it back. After reflection, he muttered, 'Have you served this notice on her?'

'No, not yet. She's had a good read, though. Elita plans to consult the family lawyer. She says her family will take this to a tribunal. If it goes to that stage, it will be the finish her career. Whether she wins or loses — it will be over for her before it even starts. And she could be the finest Detective Superintendent the Met has ever had. Do you want that?'

'The bastards. It's not fair. They're using Elita to get to me, aren't they? How do I get her out of this shit? She's done nothing wrong... It's me that they're after. And they're using her as the bait...'

'Now you're talking sense. I can help. But I need your support.'

72

Just after 7:20 pm, I arrived at Inspector Beedi's semi-detached home in Sherman Way — just off our ground.

Mrs. Beedi came to the front door. She appeared to be a tight-laced woman aged about forty years with good teeth.

'Yes?' she said.

'I am Sergeant Chesterfield. I have come to see Mr. Beedi. Is he in?'

'May I ask the reason for your visit? He went off duty several hours ago.'

'Tell him it's about P.C. Ruff Palmerston.'

She pushed the door half-closed and padded away in her slippers to find her husband. A little later, Mr. Beedi arrived at the door dressed in shirtsleeves, with cuffs rolled to the elbows. He'd apparently been doing the washing-up. 'What is it, Chesterfield? I do not like being disturbed at home. This better be good.'

'Oh, yes, sir, it is. Can I come in?'

'Yes, very well. I suppose you will have to,' Mr. Beedi pointed to the drawing-room. 'Better go in there.'

'Does the Sergeant want tea or coffee?' Mrs. Beedi called from the kitchen.

'No dear, he doesn't require either because he's not staying long —' Then the Inspector turned to me and added: 'Are you, Sergeant?'

'No, sir.'

'Take a seat. Explain.'

I took a deep breath. Then fixed him in the eye. 'If I could get rid of Ruff Palmerston *right now* — would that get Elita off the disciplinary allegations that you've made?'

'It depends. What are you planning?'

'If I could convince Ruff to step down *right now*, tonight, promise to resign this very evening. If I could get his signature right *now*. Would that be enough to save Elita's skin?'

'That would be sufficient, *yes*. But how would you get him to resign? Ruff isn't going anywhere. He's made it very clear that he'll have to be pushed. I asked Paddy Gallaher to get rid of him twelve months ago, and even *he* failed. What makes you think you have any better chance than Paddy? Given that you're still wet behind the ears — for God's sake! You're still a probationary Sergeant. While Paddy Gallaher is the most experienced Skipper on division and even *he* couldn't achieve the impossible. Ruff is clever and cunning. He'll play you like he's played Gallaher and me... and all the other supervisors he's ever met. He's as slippery as a snake in a soap-bowl. You'll never get any shit on him.'

'If I got him to resign tonight — if I get him to sign his 728 of resignation in front of you, witnessed by you — would that get rid of the complaint against Elita?'

'Witnessed by me?'

'Yes. I have Ruff outside right now. We can do this *tonight*.'

Beedi looked out of the window to see if he might catch a glimpse of the Constable. 'What are you saying?' he asked.

'A deal. A trade-off. I will offer you the head of Ruff in exchange for Elita's career. What do you say?'

'I agree. But only if Ruff resigns *tonight*. I'm not having that ruffian in my house though...'

'We will do the messy business by the car, then...'

'Sergeant Chesterfield is leaving...' shouted Inspector Beedi.

'That *was* a short visit!' returned his wife.

'I'm just accompanying him to this car, dear.'

We stepped outside. We stepped towards the rusty heap of a Hillman that sat disconsolately at the kerbside. Inside was an unmistakable shape, the tiny head and colossal gut of Constable Ruff Palmerston. He dragged on a ciggie and fiddled with his lighter. Inspector Beedi and I stepped closer towards the car. Ruff rolled down the window, and a thick wave of smoke emerged.

'Evening Inspector,' said the Constable.

'Well?' Beedi said.

'On the date specified on the Form 163 that I am about to serve,' I verbalized, 'It is alleged that you P.C. Palmerston entered a licenced premises while on duty in uniform — the Crown public house — and there you purchased a bottle of intoxicating liquor. A dark green bottle of Q.C. Cream Sherry, in fact. That is an offence under the Licensing Act. An offence you are familiar with. You are not obliged to say anything unless you wish to do so, but anything you do say may be taken down in writing and given in evidence. Do you remember the time, Ruff? On our quick changeover day?'

Ruff looked at me with guilty eyes.

'What do you want to say?' Inspector Beedi snorted.

'Please accept this letter of resignation from the Force.' Ruff responded. 'I already prepared it. I typed it onto a form 728. I haven't signed it yet. Because the Sarge said that you might want to witness my signature.'

'Do you have a pen?' Beedi asked. I produced my black ballpoint, and Ruff scribbled his signature onto the form in the Inspector's presence, using the car door handle as a flat surface.

'Give me...' said the Inspector. He grabbed the signed letter of resignation and scrutinized it. And after he read-it-over, he said: 'Constable Palmerston. As a result of this, you are officially suspended from duty. Do you have your warrant card with you?'

Ruff took the precious card from his pocket and handed it over.

'It will take at least two weeks to get the writing done. So, take a fortnight's special leave. Stay at home. Do not try to contact any *other* officer expect Sergeant Chesterfield or me. Do you understand?'

'Yes, sir.'

'Well, get away with you then. I will get the Sergeant to call on you in due course. To organize your departure. Right?'

'Yes, sir.'

'Great work Clarence. I will see you in my office Monday. And we'll get the paperwork completed together. You've done something today that Paddy could never achieve.'

'Yes, sir.' It was the first time the Inspector had praised me since I'd arrived on 'Q' Division. I was about to walk to the passenger door when I realized I still had one more task to complete. I turned to face Beedi and took Elita's folded Form 163 from my shirt pocket. 'I never had the opportunity to serve this on her,' I told him.

'Give it here then, and I'll handle it right now,' replied Beedi.

'Sure,' I said.

He ripped the form into tiny bits and allowed it to flutter to the ground.

EPILOGUE

One evening in March 1976, I was posted to the wireless car — call sign Quebec Six — for late-turn duty.

I was posted as the radio operator. Elita drove. She'd managed to pass the Hendon Advanced Course at Christmas. They searched for an urgent replacement for Ruff when he got the tintack. She was the obvious choice. The most capable and gifted officer we had. Ruff went North with his wife. To work in the launderette business.

After his resignation, I made a life-changing decision. I decided to give up my stripes. I could no longer — in good conscience — be a supervisor at Quebec Mike. I needed to learn to be a good copper before I tried again to be a supervisor. I needed to go back to the basics of coppering. And Elita was the one to teach me.

I left the Section House in the New Year and now lived in the hayloft above Elita's stables. This meant we saw much more of each other if you know what I mean.

Anyway, on that evening in March, we cruised down King's Drive. It was about nine o'clock, and we saw a dark shape emerge from a shadowy doorway at the Masonic Lodge. 'Pull in here,' I suggested.

Elita pulled the Blue Rover P6 into the kerbside. We watched as a chap emerged from the Lodge and into the streetlight. He was wearing a suit and shiny black shoes, and he looked up and down the street in a shifty manner. He held a slim briefcase in one hand and a sizeable brown-red bag in the other. Once he was satisfied that no one was about, the character went over to a silver Granada that was parked by a bus stop. He settled the maroon bag on the ground and began to fiddle with a set of car keys. He dropped the keys onto the pavement and swayed as he bent to pick them up.

'That's Inspector Beedi's car, isn't it?' said Elita.

'Yup.'

'Is that Beedi?'

'I think so.'

'He's pissed. He's reeling... '

'Yep. Looks like he is.'

'What's in that bag?'

'His accordion.'

'His what?'

'A concertina.'

'What's that?' she said.

It was too late to explain. And anyway, the figure had slid into the front seat of the Ford and started the engine.

'Give him a little space...' I told Elita. 'Let him get ahead. Then we'll follow.'

'Yes, dear.'

We watched the silver car move off, and Elita purred the Rover forwards. We allowed his car to get ahead — then we started to tail him from a distance.

'Where's he going?' Elita asked.

'Probably back home...' I said. 'Just off our ground. To Sherman Way, I guess...'

'Did you see that?' she interrupted.

I did. The nearside rear tyre of his Ford touched a kerbstone. There's nothing particularly noteworthy in that, you might think, and it was not something that might be recognized by any ordinary copper. But Elita was no ordinary copper. She was extraordinary. And she knew that that brush against the sidewall was sufficient grounds to pull him over. That little mishap was all we needed to demand that the driver take a roadside breath test.

'That was enough, wasn't it?'

'Sure was.'

'Let's give him a tug. Stick a tube in his gob.'

'Good idea.' I hit the blue lamp, and Elita flashed the headlights. But the silver Granada didn't slow down or stop.

'Give him a blast or two of the two-tones,' Elita suggested.

I gave him a three-second burst. If anything, the car started to quicken.

'Shit,' I exclaimed. 'I think we've got a chase.' I picked up the R/T microphone: 'M.P. M.P. from Quebec Six. Please note: Silver Ford Granada Romeo, Romeo, November Eight-Two-Nine, Mike. Failing to stop for the police. Currently heading north on King's Drive, Quebec Mike section.'

'Received Quebec Six. Keep up the commentary...'

'Still headed North on King's Drive. Towards Quebec Bravo section. Speed fifty in a thirty limit.'

'Roger. Keep the commentary going.'

'Now left, left, left into Panama Way... Stand by.'

We saw the Granada move to the side and slow down a bit. He wanted us to pass. But we pulled behind. When we came to a complete halt — the Ford made off once more. This time at greater speed. He was trying to shake us off. What a shithead. Now he was giving it some serious welly.

'Fuck, yeah...' I shouted. 'M.P. Still on the move. Panama Way. Speeds of sixty plus. He's all over the road, M.P.' We saw the Ford slide sideways on a patch of mud, probably left by a tractor. 'Watch out for that shit...' I shouted to Elita.

'I got it,' she said. She expertly manoeuvred the wireless car around the hazard.

Then the out-of-control Ford Granada hit the oil and spun. It mounted the verge then went down a gulley. The driver did his best to roar onto the road again, but the rear wheels slipped in deep mud, and the car came to a sticky halt. We saw the driver open his door and grab for the brown bag. He started to leg it. Before I had a chance to call on the radio, Elita was on her toes. After him.

'M.P. M.P. Vehicle stopped. Driver decamped on foot. Panama Way. This is now a foot-chase. Requesting a dog unit to this location.'

'Received. Continue the foot-chase on the P.R. link. All units Quebec Mike section. Suspect decamped on foot in Panama Way. Any dog unit respond?'

'Quebec Zero.'

'Quebec Zero received. Show you assigned.'

I did my best to catch-up with Elita. But, as usual, she was way-ahead

The suspect arrived at a barbed-wire fence that separated the grass verge with a large cattle-field. He looked around, then picked his way across some cruel spikes. Elita almost reached him. When he saw her getting close, he swung his prized bag around his head and slung it at her, as forcefully as he could manage — perhaps in a vain attempt to slow her a bit. But the bag fell short, and the instrument inside let out a long, melancholy sigh.

The suspect snagged his jacket on a nasty bit of barb, but he managed to break free before Elita grabbed his arm. Once he was over the fence, he made a run for it across muddy fields.

Elita carefully negotiated the wicked spikes. She made sure she didn't snag her uniform on them and, once she'd crossed over, she resumed the chase on foot. She pursued him like a shadowing leopard.

I arrived at the steel fence a little later. I warily stepped over it. Elita was now merely a couple of yards from Beedi. Once I crossed the fence, I ran a few feet forwards. Then paused to enjoy the sight of Elita taking him down.

She pulled his legs away with a superior rugby tackle. His face slammed into the dirt, and his chin came to rest in a stinking cow-pat. By the time I arrived, Elita had him trapped tightly between those celebrated thighs. 'He isn't going anywhere now. Are you sweetie-pie?' she proclaimed. The man merely groaned.

'May I do the honours?' I asked.

'Of course, you can, honey-cake,' Elita said, with a smile.

'Mr. Beedi...' I continued. 'I'm arresting you for failing to stop for police, for reckless driving and for driving while unfit. You are not obliged to say anything — but anything you do say may be taken down in writing and given in evidence. What do you want to say?'

'Humph...' was his reply, so Elita increased pressure on his chest with her thigh-lock.

'M.P. M.P. One male detained. In a cow field by Panama Way. I request a van unit to our position on the hurry-up and handcuffs. Dog no longer required. Please advise Quebec Bravo that we will be bringing this prisoner into *their* charge room...'

'Roger that. Confirm you want to take the prisoner to Quebec Bravo? For your info, our maps here at I.R. show your current position to be Quebec Mike. So, this prisoner ought to be going to Quebec Mike police station, for your info, over...'

'Received M.P. But he will *have* to be taken to Quebec Bravo. The prisoner is a serving police officer currently attached to Quebec Mike. We need to take him to a neutral station.'

'Roger that, and understood here at I.R. We will comment to that effect on the log and get the back-hall Inspector to review this end and contact A.10 on your behalf. We have the commentary taped for your evidence.'

'Thanks. Please keep the tape safe. There is no doubt the conduct of this officer has been disgraceful...'

'Received and understood,' said the Information Room operator. 'Bringing the Force into disrepute. All understood. Out to you.'

Please take a moment to add a review of this book on Amazon

The author reads all reviews and takes them seriously. He uses the feedback to improve his stories

73

GLOSSARY

Glossary

Here's a handy list of period-**authentic** Cockney Slang and **genuine** 1970's Police Jargon used by Ruff and his team-mates in this story.

Most of the police **jargon** and abbreviations used here are no longer in everyday use. And, it's worth mentioning that some of the slang used on the streets in the 1970's has been updated since because Cockney is an ever-evolving and constantly-changing language. For example, Ayrton Senna (the slang for a tenner) was *never* used in the Seventies by Ruff and his mates because the racing driver wasn't known in Britain until 1983. Similarly, the slang introduced into British conversational vernacular by characters from the T.V. sitcom 'Only Fools and Horses' — words such as plonker, jubbly and cushty — only became popular *after* the airing of the show in 1981. Also, some of the Cockney terms used in that TV show, for example, Kermit the Frog (for bog) were very rarely used by 'real' Cockneys on the streets.

A10, police procedure, noun: The Police Complaints and Discipline Department. Later A10 became C.I.B.2 and more even more recently: The Directorate of Professional Standards (DPS)

A4, police procedure, noun: Women's Police Unit. All departments of the Commissioner's Office [C.O.] had letters attached to them in the 1970s. Broadly speaking: A department was 'Admin', B department was 'Traffic', C department was 'Crime', D department was 'Training' and F department was 'Finance.' Thus, the department of A4 was the Women's Branch. A4 was disbanded by Commander Daphne Skillern in 1974 after new legislation brought about equality in the workplace

Anthony Blunt, noun, also Sir Anthony. Blunt was a well-known and much despised traitor so Cockney Londoners used his name as rhyming slang to replace the [much worse] vulgar word for a woman's genitals. It seems appropriate. The word was also used to describe an unpleasant character... or an idiot

Aylesbury Duck, vulgar slang: Fuck, to fuck

B department, police procedure, noun: Traffic

Betty Grables, noun: Tables

Billy Bunters, noun: Punters i.e. gamblers, speculators or customers

Bin lids, noun : Kids, children

Blacks Rats, colloquial pejorative expression: Traffic patrols, traffic officers

Boat-race, noun: Face

Bread and honey, bread, noun: Money

Bristols, noun: Bristol Cities, titties, breasts

Brown Bread, noun: Dead. 'Hovis' (a well-known English bread bakery that specialized in baking brown bread) also means the same thing.

Bubble and Squeak, noun: Greek

Butchers, Butchers Hook, verb : Look

C.M.O. acronym: Chief Medical Officer

C.O. acronym: Commissioner's Office [normally referred to as Scotland Yard by the press and public — though *always* referred to as C.O. by Met officers.]

C.V.I. acronym: Central Vehicle Index, a card index for vehicles registration before the arrival of the Computer Terminal Bureau [CTB.] It took months to come fully on line. This was before the Police National Computer became reliable in about 1976.

Cattle-trucked, vulgar slang: Fucked, knackered, exhausted

Cockle and hen, number: ten

Cream-crackered, adjective: Knackered, extremely tired also used as 'Jacobs'— Jacobs was a well-known Irish/English cracker-biscuit manufacturer

Creeping insects, colloquial pejorative expression for detectives, from the abbreviation: C.I.D. or creeping insects department

Currant Bun, the, noun: Sun

Dee for Pee, police slang: Discount for Police

Dicky Bird, noun: Word

Drum, drums, noun: House, home, lodging

Dunlop Tyre (English spelling for Tire), noun: Liar

Early Worm, idiom: Early turn, the earliest shift of the day

Elephant's Trunk, adjective and noun: Drunk

Fatacc, acronym police procedure: Fatal Accident — from the teleprinter code

Fisherman's Daughter, noun, water

Gaff, Irish slang noun for dwelling house

Gander, thieves slang: Look

Germans, German Bands, noun: Hands

Ginger Beer, adjective: Queer, 1970s pejorative term for gay

Giraffe, verb : Laugh

Gold Watch, noun: Scotch, whisky

Grocers, noun, police slang: Those accused of Gross Indecency

Half-inched, verb: Pinched, to pinch, to steal

Hovis, adjective: as in 'Brown bread'

I.R.B. police procedure, acronym: Incident Report Book

Jack and Danny, noun: Fanny, vagina

Jam jars, Jam jar, noun: Cars, car

J Bells, police procedural, the 'alarm' that rings on a teleprinter when an urgent message comes into the station — during the Cold War

Jimmy, Jimmy Riddle, verb: Piddle, to urinate

Judges Rules, noun: The caution read out to a suspect upon arrest, before P.A.C.E. was introduced

Kettle and Hob, Kettle, noun: Fob i.e. wristwatch

L.A.S. acronym: London Ambulance Service

L.F.B. acronym: London Fire Brigade

Lah-Di-Dah, noun: Star, also used for cigar

Love and Kisses, informal noun, Missus

Misper, acronym: Missing Person — from the teleprinter code

MP, police procedural term: The 'call sign' for Information Room at Scotland Yard. Now incoming calls are handled by C.C.C. and dispatched by them. Though a small 'I.R.' is maintained at C.C.C. Lambeth and supervised by S.I.s

North, North and South, noun: mouth

One-unders, colloquial expression: person on a rail track, often suicidal

Quack, noun: a pretender to some medical skill

Peeping Tom, police jargon: A male voyeur. Taken from the story of Lady Godiva

Pikey, pikeys, pejorative expression: Travelers, members of the gypsy community

Plonk, plonks, noun: pejorative term for Woman Police Constable, commonly used in the 1970's

Pony, Pony and Trap, noun: Crap, excreta

Porky-pied, Porky Pie, Porky, verb: Lied, to lie

Q Boat, police slang, for a 'plain wrapper' undercover police car, also known as a 'Q car' in the Met. Each division had at least one Q boat or Q car, always driven by an experienced 'Class One' driver and crewed by a detective constable and plain-clothes Sergeant. Named after the special service/mystery ships of the First and Second World Wars. In the Shepherd's Bush murders of 1966 the F division 'Q Boat' call-sign 'Foxtrot One On' had been patrolling East Acton when officers spotted a suspicious vehicle in Braybrook Street. The driver was recognized to be a known criminal and the 'Q boat' police started to question him. His front seat passenger, Harry Roberts, produced a Luger and, with his back seat accomplice John Duddy, he shot dead all three officers. The name 'Harry Roberts' was often used during the Seventies to taunt police

Q.P.M. acronym: Queen's Police Medal

Quack, noun, doctor or surgeon

Radio Rental, noun: Mental

Raspberry tart, noun and verb: Fart, to fart, to break wind

RC4, police procedure: Race Code, RC4 is Indian, or anyone from the Indian sub-continent. Race Codes were used before Identity Codes. More recently, self-defined ethnicity codes have been introduced (S.D.E. codes) for the British Police Service.

Reg Varney, noun: Pakistani

Relief, police procedural term: The uniform team on shift work

Rosy Lee, rosy or Rosie, noun: Tea

Rub-A-Dub, noun: Pub, public house

Ruby Murray, noun: Curry

Saucepan-lids, noun: Kids, children

Schtum, criminal slang, adjective, silent or non-communicative

Score, noun: twenty nicker [bits] i.e. twenty pounds sterling, or two cockles

Scotch eggs, noun: Legs

Silvery Moon, noun: pejorative term: Coon, insulting term for a black person

Skin and the blister, noun : Sister

Sky-rocket (s), noun: pocket

Smudger, noun: Photographer, normally amateur

Song-and-dance, noun: Chance

Sprogs, slang noun: Children

Stewart Granger, noun, danger

Stuck On, adjective: to be stuck on the dab, reported for discipline offences

Sweeney Todd, noun: Flying Squad, London's robbery squad

T.D.A. acronym: Taking [and] Driving Away, these days it's known as 'Unauthorised Taking of a Motor Vehicle' or 'TWOC' which means Taking without Owners Consent

Taters, Taters in the Mold, adjective: Cold

Tea-leafed, noun, can be used as a verb: Thieved, thief

Thrupennys, Thrupenny Bits, noun: Tits, breasts

Tit-for-tat, noun: Hat

Tommy tank, verb: Wank, masturbate

Trouble, noun: Trouble and strife, wife

Wooden top, woodentops: colloquial pejorative expression for uniform 'branch' — named after the children's television show puppets, 1955

Woolly Woofter, informal, offensive, pejorative slang for poof hence: poofter

Questions or suggestions: Tweet the author @neilmach

74

LISA'S CANN'S COCKNEY EXERCISES

Lisa's Cockney Exercises

Have you enjoyed the authentic London cockney slang used in this book? Do want to learn more? Try the exercises below to improve your everyday Cockney lingo. With thanks to the communications officers at the police communications command center at C.C.C. Bow, East London, who assisted me with this compilation. And in loving memory of Bow Operator Lisa Cann who asked me to compile this list for her.

'With Plates like that you could never join the Rozz – they're as flat as a pair of pancakes'
    'That's not a bint, officer, that lady is my dear trouble, the China'
    'My fence will give you a monkey for a stash like that'
    'We'll give these two teas a tickle before we go in for Rosie'
    'After lates we'll go for a ruby — so you'll need a score with you or maybe a pony if you want more than a pig's ear.'
    'Get in the van cuz. So we can spin your titfer'

'Give the bint a cup of Rosie to stop all her bunny, she's doing my uncle in'

'Good grief, skip, it's bloody tators out 'ere tonight'

'He got clobbered over the uncle by one of them riot cozzers'

'He's been on his tod since his trouble ran off with a Harry Nash geezer from the down the docks.'

'I felt well tom 'n' dick after that slag tea-leafed my stash'

'I got this new whistle and daisies for my week at the Big House'

'I will be with you in a minute Sarge, just going for a tom tit'

'Yes sir, I will get on the blower for a sherbet, for your brass'

'I'm going down the battle to score more gear'

'I'm off to the big house in the morning- I'll probably get bird'

'Keep your Germans away from your Dickie skyrockets, you slag'

'My idiot bin got his jam jar twocked this weekend. I told him not to leave it in the frog'

'My bin-lid is up the rub a dub at the moment, silly cow'

'My currant is just a little tea leaf officer, not a blagger'

'My gaff got screwed last week. The tea-leaf nicked my bin's stash'

'My jam got pranged outside the battle, you know, the one up the frog by the quack's?'

'My old man blagged our ma'am for her dog'

'One is a well-known Tom. The other looks like her bin lid'

'Sarge, he had the gear stuffed inside his rhythms'

'She's on her Jack at the moment on account of her iffy boat. On the plus-side, at least she ain't radio rental'

'Shut your north – let me do the talking'

'Sorry Guv, I lost the stash and it's all gone Pete Tong.'

'Sorry Skip, I am just on the Tex Ritter. Out in a few shakes'

'That bint is up the duff and my stupid currant is responsible'

'This tom ain't worth half a monkey'

'The Rozz have got a double-ya out on you, so expect a knock at your gaff any time soon'

'This gear is worth a couple of ton but nowhere near a monkey'

'This slag came up and tea-leafed my dosh right under my bloody I suppose'

'Wooden tops won't find much, but the filth will fit you up'

'I fancy a pigs, shall we go up the battle for a couple of sherbets?'

'I would like to go for a Ruby tonight but I am totally brassic (boracic)'

'After three night shifts I'm completely creamed'

'Are you having a giraffe? This stash ain't worth a pony'

'Are you mutton? I said show us your Germans, you slag'

'Careful — those blaggers might be tooled'

'Don't forget to take his daisies off before putting him in the bin'

'Don't worry, the rozz will never stop her, she's just a bin lid'

'Empty your sky rockets on the bonnet please, sir'

'Gaw, his almond's don't half pen'

'Have a butchers over that wall, take your titfer off first…Sir Anthony…'

'He got his Hampstead's knocked out last weekend'

'He's got a red gang scarf around his Gregory'

'He's the neighborhood Nonce and a smudger to boot'

'He put his size nine daisies straight through the living room door'

'He's not *real* filth Nan, he works with the Feds at Stokey. But actually he's one of their Strawberry's'

'I apologize officer, my old lady can be a right soppy bint at times'

'I got some baccy already but I need to go up the frog for more Vera's'

'I called the Rozz because of terrible pen in the flat above. And it is getting worse'

'I found a joint in his top right sky rocket, didn't I Sarge?'

'I know that boat Sarge — it belongs to a blagger from last week's Gazette'

'I met my future trouble outside the Lillian shop up the Mile End'

'I parked my jam-jar on the frog outside my skin's drum. That's where I last saw it, officer, on my old China's life, bless 'er'

'I went to the fence with that dog and got myself a pony'

'I will go down the factory in the morning and report things, keep your Barnet on'

'I'm Hank, let's go for a quick Ruby'

'I'll get on the blower first thing, officer'

'I'm sorry constable, but my trouble is slightly Brahms on account of it's her birthday. The silly bint'

'I'm up before the beak in the morning. I need to get my Uncle down'

'Hello, police? I'm reporting I lost my dog in a battle last night'

'If he's *really* filth then he ought to show you his brief'

'If he still has the gear on him, it will be stuffed down his daisies'

'Then he gave me a kick straight in the Jacobs, officer'

'If you're going down the Lillian shop get us a couple of Joes and a gherkin'

'Keep your minces open for five-o while we hide the stash'

'My best China is doing a five stretch at Scrubs'

'Scrubs? My bin lid is doing 12 months bird in that clink too. She's my bricks and I'm so proud of 'er... she's been done for hammering a nonce'

'My bricks got a new pair of daisies down Petticoat Lane – they only cost 'er a pony because of 'er small plates'

'My brother in law is in the filth at West Hendon. I'll ask him'

'My current lost his Aristotle after collecting a cue in the boat at the rub-a-dub on the corner'

'My old lady says she's up the duff again, silly bint'

'My old man is up the Mile End, in a battle at the moment'

'My skin got a new titfer up west.'

'No officer that is me China's drum, *my gaff* is down Homerton way'

'One of my bin lids is a proper little tea leaf'

'Sarge, he had it on his dancers long before we got there'

'Sarge, what's the S.P. on this villain?' 'He's a well-known nonce'

'Call a plonk. This bint keeps her stash up her Jack and Danny'

'Show us your Germans – keep 'em out of your skies'

'Shtum, *shtum*, there are feds all over. Those two are giving us a long butchers. The one in the fancy jam on the other side of the frog'

'Stop your bunny and help me hide this iffy gear will ya?'

'That dog isn't worth a pony. I can offer you five sovs max'

'That jam-jar is red hot – leave it well alone'

'That's an exxy battle –an Aristotle of pigs will cost you a Lady'

'The bint with the large Bristols has the stash hid in her skies'

'The blaggers got away in a red jam-jar Sarge... index to follow'

'The blaggers left their shooters behind in the gaff'

'The filth are casing our drums at the moment, we'll go up West'

'The geezer with the long Barnet just got out of a silver jam'

'The pen and ink was from a bint upstairs. She's probably been Hovis over a week, according to the Police quack'

'The Rozz will spin your strides, so it's best to stuff your gear in your daisies'

'The Kermit is through the door and up the apples – first door on the left'

'The woodentops came around Sunday to spin our gaff'

'A couple of brasses hang out on the corner at Homerton High Street every evening'

'There'll be a large gold watch in this for you — if you keep your North and South schtum'

'Those slags are also well-known for fencing hot dogs'

'Use your loaf when filth are around. Keep your mince pies peeled'

'We're just gonna give your jam-jar a spin, son – routine stop and all that. Keep your German's where we can see them'

'We'll blag our way into the club with a brief'

'We have a stash of iffy handbags here, Sarge'

'When you go up the frog later would you get me today's currant – for the form'

'Yes guv, I was sat watching telly in me Jack's when two slags broke in me gaff and helped themselves to a monkey plus my best gold watch... The Anthony Blunts'

'Yes officer, the John had it on his dancers... and he took my monkey with him'

Help required?

Tweet the author @neilmach for answers or comments

ABOUT THE AUTHOR

Printed in Great Britain
by Amazon